THE TURBULENT 60s

1965

Terrie Petree, *Book Editor*

Bruce Glassman, *Vice President*
Bonnie Szumski, *Publisher*
Scott Barbour, *Managing Editor*
David M. Haugen, *Series Editor*

**GREENHAVEN
PRESS ®**

THOMSON
─────✳─────™
GALE

San Diego • Detroit • New York • San Francisco • Cleveland
New Haven, Conn. • Waterville, Maine • London • Munich

LIBRARY OF CONGRESS CATALOGING-IN-PUBLICATION DATA

1965 / Terrie Petree, book editor.
   p. cm. — (The turbulent 60s)
Includes bibliographical references and index.
ISBN 0-7377-1508-1 (lib. bdg. : alk. paper) —
ISBN 0-7377-1509-X (pbk. : alk. paper)
   1. United States—History—1961–1969—Sources. 2. Nineteen sixty-five, A.D.—Sources. I. Petree, Terrie. II. Series.
E846.A18 2004
973.923—dc21
                                                         2003053927

CONTENTS

The 1960s were a period of immense change in America. What many view as the complacency of the 1950s gave way to increased radicalism in the 1960s. The newfound activism of America's youth turned an entire generation against the social conventions of their parents. The rebellious spirit that marked young adulthood was no longer a stigma of the outcast but rather a badge of honor among those who wanted to remake the world. And in the 1960s, there was much to rebel against in America. The nation's involvement in Vietnam was one of the catalysts that helped galvanize young people in the early 1960s. Another factor was the day-to-day Cold War paranoia that seemed to be the unwelcome legacy of the last generation. And for black Americans in particular, there was the inertia of the civil rights movement that, despite seminal victories in the 1950s, had not effectively countered the racism still plaguing the country. All of these concerns prompted the young to speak out, to decry the state of the nation that would be their inheritance.

The 1960s, then, may best be remembered for its spirit of confrontation. The student movement questioned American imperialism, militant civil rights activists confronted their elders over the slow progress of change, and the flower children faced the nation's capitalistic greed and conservative ethics and opted to create a counterculture. There was a sense of immediacy to all this activism, and people put their bodies on the line to bring about change. Although there were reactionaries and conservative holdouts, the general feeling was that a united spirit of resistance could stop the inevitability of history. People could shape their own destinies, and together they could make a better world. As sixties chronicler Todd Gitlin writes, "In the Sixties it seemed especially true that History with a capital H had come down to earth, either interfering with life or making it possible: and that within History, or threaded through it, people were living with a supercharged density: lives were bound up with one another, making claims on one another, drawing one another into the common project."

Perhaps not everyone experienced what Gitlin describes, but few would argue that the nation as a whole was left untouched by the radical notions of the times. The women's movement, the civil rights movement, and the antiwar movement left indelible marks. Even the hippie movement left behind a relaxed morality and a more ecological mindset. Popular culture, in turn, reflected these changes: Music became more diverse and experimental, movies adopted more adult themes, and fashion attempted to replicate the spirit of uninhibited youth. It seemed that every facet of American culture was affected by the pervasiveness of revolution in the 1960s, and despite the diversity of rebellions, there remained a sense that all were related to, as Gitlin puts it, "the common project."

Of course, this communal zeitgeist of the 1960s is best attributed to the decade in retrospect. The 1960s were not a singular phenomenon but a progress of individual days, of individual years. Greenhaven Press follows this rubric in The Turbulent Sixties series. Each volume of this series is devoted to the major events that define a specific year of the decade. The events are discussed in carefully chosen articles. Some of these articles are written by historians who have the benefit of hindsight, but most are contemporary accounts that reveal the complexity, confusion, excitement, and turbulence of the times. Each article is prefaced by an introduction that places the event in its historical context. Every anthology is also introduced by an essay that gives shape to the entire year. In addition, the volumes in the series contain time lines, each of which gives an at-a-glance structure to the major events of the topic year. A bibliography of helpful sources is also provided in each anthology to offer avenues for further study. With these tools, readers will better understand the developments in the political arena, the civil rights movement, the counterculture, and other facets of American society in each year. And by following the trends and events that define the individual years, readers will appreciate the revolutionary currents of this tumultuous decade—the turbulent sixties.

Year of Outcry

In 1965 the shaky silence of a nation rocked by the events of an increasingly turbulent decade was shattered. As the conflict in Vietnam escalated into full-scale warfare and the civil rights movement gained momentum despite violent opposition, the men and women of America began to cry out. They carried placards in the streets, burned their draft cards, marched on southern capitals, wrote books, made speeches, and gave their lives trying to make their voices heard. This cacophony of voices permeated the American conscience, insisting that citizens consider not only the prevailing demands of war and racial equality, but also the needs of those who were just beginning to join the outcry. Like a cracking mirror, each issue splintered into numberless smaller issues, and each smaller issue reflected a faction of Americans struggling to gain or preserve their rights. The war in Vietnam aroused antiwar and anti-Communist protests; the civil rights movement provoked demonstrations for voters' rights, peaceful resistance, and legalized segregation. In 1965 freedom of speech was no longer just a constitutional right, but a rite of passage for every minority, special-interest group, or average American who wanted to rise up from the silence and be heard. From farmers to feminists, the clamor of American voices roared for liberty and justice for all.

Vietnam

Of all the dissonant voices in 1965, the loudest were those who spoke out either for or against the war in Vietnam. President Lyndon B. Johnson's decision to engage in complete warfare against Communist forces in Vietnam divided the nation in half. Some Americans believed that the United States bore a moral obligation to stop the spread of communism. Others felt that the act of war itself was immoral. Throughout the year, both sides took to the streets to express their opinions about the newly declared war in Vietnam.

From sit-ins on the East Coast to marches on the University of California at Berkeley campus, students were particularly vocal in expressing their antiwar sentiments. In the assessment of historians Nancy Zaroulis and Gerald Sullivan, many of these students feared "that the war in Vietnam would somehow get out of hand and catapult the country—and the world—into the final nuclear holocaust."[1] Organized into powerful and outspoken protest organizations, groups like the Student Nonviolent Coordinating Committee (SNCC) facilitated nationwide antiwar activity. In March students and educators at New York University staged one of the first "teach-ins," a revolutionary form of protest which involved conference-style discussions of the war in Vietnam. In May students at Columbia protested the war by interrupting an NROTC (Naval Reserve Officers Training Corps) awards ceremony at the university. The student protest movement was especially active at Berkeley where students participated in teach-ins, sit-ins, and marches against the U.S. presence in Vietnam. In the spring of 1965 Berkeley students held the first Vietnam Day devoted to promoting awareness of the U.S. role in Vietnam. Singers such as Joan Baez and Phil Ochs sang protest songs and helped to rally student sympathy for the protest movement.

While student demonstrations kept the antiwar outcry at the forefront of American awareness in 1965, it was the furor against the draft that incited the most dramatic of these protests. On November 2, 1965, Norman Morrison, resident of a Quaker community in Baltimore and the father of three young children, soaked himself in kerosene and lit himself on fire in protest against the war in Vietnam. Although Morrison had participated in several antiwar demonstrations, he felt powerless against the continued violence in Vietnam and the ratification of draft legislation. Morrison's act of self-immolation shocked Americans, not only became he took his own life, but because he did so on the steps of the Pentagon in full view of Secretary of Defense Robert McNamara's window, and he brought his one-year-old daughter with him. Morrison's daughter, Emily, survived the fire, but all who witnessed the immolation, either on the steps of the Pentagon or in pictures and television reports, were affected by Morrison's desperate need to cry out against the Vietnam War.

In a preemptive measure to counterbalance the backlash against the declaration of war in Vietnam, President Johnson unveiled his plans for the "Great Society." Mirroring the growing success of President John F. Kennedy's Peace Corps pilot program, the Great Society included programs for education, welfare, and social reform. For example, the Job Corps was designed to provide underprivileged young adults with the education and skills necessary to enter the workforce. The Great Society also pledged greater federal support to the arts and showed this support by hosting the first White House Festival of the Arts. However, the Job Corps, the Festival of the Arts, and other programs were all affected by the shouts of dissatisfaction that the president had hoped the Great Society would quiet.

Advancing Civil Rights

Aside from the protests surrounding the Vietnam War, the loudest shouts were those of civil rights leaders and demonstrators. In a speech delivered to the Howard University graduating class of 1965, President Johnson urged African American students to further the cause of equality by working hard and setting good examples. Although he expressed support for the cause, he also warned students that the fight for justice was an uphill battle that would rest mainly on their own shoulders. Actively shouldering his own share of the burden was civil rights leader Martin Luther King Jr. In early 1965 he garnered support for the Voting Rights Act by leading demonstrators and activists to register voters throughout the South.

As part of this movement, King led a group of supporters, writers, movie stars, and activists on a fifty-mile march from Selma to Montgomery, Alabama. The demonstration was intended to be peaceful, but immediately met violent opposition from white Alabama residents. The march was originally scheduled to take place in early February but was called off several times because Alabama governor George Wallace refused to protect the marchers and sanctioned the use of police force to prevent the demonstration. On Sunday, March 7, 1965, a group of marchers from Marion, Alabama, began the march, led by Reverend Hosea L. Williams, while King was in Washington, D.C., seeking federal protection from the brutality of Governor Wallace and Alabama law enforcement agencies. Known as "Bloody Sunday," the marchers were met by a large group of state troopers as they crossed the Pettus Bridge outside Selma. The marchers were ordered to retreat from the bridge and abandon their plans to march on the capital. With tear gas and batons, the troopers then began to attack the marchers, most of whom had begun to bow in prayer.

The marchers retreated to a housing project in Selma as the troopers continued to beat them and other witnesses to the events of "Bloody Sunday." The violent attack by law enforcement officers on those attempting to peacefully protest brought immediate media attention to the small town of Selma.

The increasingly violent response to King and the protesters in Alabama evoked a powerful and sympathetic response from outraged Americans across the country and from lawmakers in Washington, D.C. Johnson spoke out against Wallace and the racism sanctioned by the Alabama government. King and the marchers were then granted federal protection on the long march from Selma to Montgomery. On March 21 over twenty-five thousand marchers began yet again in Selma, this time crossing the bloody Pettus Bridge without incident. They marched despite the rainy, cold weather and the mobs of angry agitators who stood along the side of the highway shouting obscenities and racial slurs at the peaceful protesters. The National Guard flanked the protesters along the highway during the day and circled around the camps where they slept at night to protect the marchers. Af-

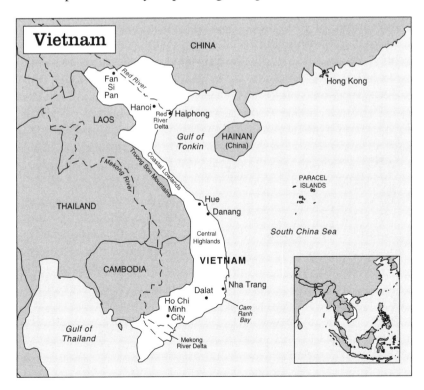

ter marching twelve miles a day for four days and sleeping outside in the rain, they arrived on March 25 to a city divided. In Montgomery, angry citizens lined the streets shouting for the protesters to get out while others waved from windows and welcomed the civil rights activists to the capital of Alabama. After several violently thwarted attempts, the long march from Selma to Montgomery was successfully completed, and as a result of the public awareness created by the march, the Voting Rights Act of 1965 was ratified by Congress just five months later.

Despite the success of the march, violence surrounding the civil rights movement was not uncommon in 1965, nor was it confined to white segregationists. During the year of outcry, another outspoken civil rights leader, Malcolm X, was assassinated by members of a rival Black Muslim organization while delivering a speech in Manhattan. His murder demonstrated the passionate response that the civil rights movement triggered in the hearts of Americans, but especially in those who suffered the most from the injustice of inequality.

Riot in the Streets

In the summer of 1965 these passions boiled over in the streets of the Watts neighborhood in Los Angeles. Watts was a black neighborhood where racial inequality translated directly into a crippling combination of joblessness, poverty, and lack of opportunity. On the hot afternoon of August 11, the tension between the Los Angeles Police Department and the residents of Watts was palpable, like a stick of dynamite waiting until the fuse was short enough to blow. When police officers began the routine arrest of a young male Watts resident, the situation quickly escalated into unforeseeable violence and destruction. Residents believed that the officers were unnecessarily forceful during the arrest and in their treatment of witnesses at the scene. Onlookers began to yell and throw small objects at the officers and within a few minutes one of the longest and most violent rebellions in U.S. history began. For six days the neighborhood was besieged by angry African Americans who looted stores and lit buildings on fire. Historian John L. Chapman recorded that the frustration of Watts residents with the status quo was so widespread that "those not actually throwing stones or looting appeared to be in favor of those who were. Both older men and women, and young boys and girls, were committing overt acts of hostility."[2] After almost four thousand arrests, nearly one thousand injuries, and thirty-four deaths, the angry rebellion subsided into a troubled calm that settled over the Watts community. In the aftermath of the riots, California governor Pat Brown formed an investigative committee to study the roots of the riot and then to devise a plan to rebuild the community and provide more employment and educational opportunities for its residents.

Striking for Minority Rights

Other minorities shared the anger over poor working conditions in the United States, but chose to cry out in different ways. Cesar Chavez led the National Farm Workers Association (NFWA), a union for Hispanic American farmworkers, in a strike to protest low wages and unsanitary living conditions imposed on migrant workers in the fertile farmlands of California. Chavez was inspired by the life of India's Mohandas Gandhi and urged NFWA members and other strikers to commit themselves to nonviolent protest: "We are engaged in another struggle for the freedom and dignity which poverty denies us. But it must not be a violent struggle, even if violence is used against us."[3] Chavez asked workers to boycott the grape harvest in September 1965 in order to peacefully demand better working conditions and higher wages. The strikers conducted their protest by traveling from one grape grower to another and picketing at their properties. Many of the replacement field hands who had accepted jobs working for the grape growers were swayed by the presence of NFWA picketers at the sites where they were working and abandoned the fields in order to ally themselves with Chavez's organization. Grape growers were incensed by the number of workers who joined the protest and by the unprecedented media attention and national support that the strike garnered. Senator Robert Kennedy visited Cesar Chavez during the grape strike and was so angered by the unfair treatment of migrant workers that he returned to Washington, D.C., and immediately began to push for federal laws that would dictate the fair treatment of laborers. There were several violent confrontations between strikers and growers, but Chavez continued to urge NFWA members to protest peacefully despite the aggression of those who wanted to break the strike. The grape strike that began in September 1965 escalated into five years of continual, nonviolent protest against unjust labor conditions for Hispanic and other minority workers in California and across the United States.

White migrant workers also suffered from an endless cycle of poverty and illness perpetuated by their rootless lives moving from one harvest to the next. Writer Truman Moore followed these nomadic workers and wrote about their difficult lives and gave voice to a group of people who had been forgotten by most of America. Like the marginalized white migrant workers, there were many forgotten voices in America that were equally insistent upon joining the outcry.

Other Voices

Advances in technology were changing the way Americans worked, traveled, and perceived the future and subsequently created a previously unknown set of social customs to adopt or cry out against. In 1965 the space race and the largest electrical blackout in U.S. history caused Americans to consider the ramifications of their growing reliance on technology. Ralph Nader, also concerned with how technological change might affect society, began to establish his reputation as an activist and politician when he published his book *Unsafe at Any Speed.* The book investigated the physical dangers of the automobile and asserted that American automobile manufacturers knowingly overlooked safety features and design flaws in order to turn larger profits.

As the automobile industry and other American corporations began to expand, women started to leave more traditional roles and find work outside the home. The growing number of professional women made the voice of the newly named "feminist" movement a powerful one. While some women identified with the feminist credo outlined in Betty Friedan's *The Feminine Mystique*, others were uncertain about how the changing role of women might adversely affect American society. In 1965 writer Marion Sanders interviewed a cross section of American women and discovered that, like all of the issues during the year of outcry, the voices of the feminist movement were as varied and different as the women behind them.

The noise of a nation trying to give voice to all of the decade's myriad concerns was deafening. From the grape fields of California to the capital of Alabama and classrooms across the country, Americans were engaged in an earnest struggle to cry out against injustice and establish a society that would allow a nation built on diversity to stand indivisible. Stirred to action by the violence in Vietnam and the battle for civil rights, Americans could not afford to sit quietly while the nation reinvented itself. The greatest challenge for Americans in 1965, and during all of the turbulent sixties, was learning to discern which voices represented the most pertinent issues of the time. Some of the voices, like those shouting for peace, equality among races and genders, and fair working conditions, were so loud and insistent that they penetrated the din and demanded immediate attention. America still hears those voices today.

Notes

1. Nancy Zaroulis and Gerald Sullivan, *Who Spoke Up? American Protest Against the War in Vietnam 1963–1975.* Garden City, NY: Doubleday, 1984, p. 44.

2. John L. Chapman, *Incredible Los Angeles.* New York: Harper and Row, 1976, p. 115.

3. Quoted in Jacques E. Levy, *Cesar Chavez: Autobiography of La Causa.* New York: W.W. Norton, 1975, p. 184.

President Johnson Americanizes the Vietnam War

By Larry Berman

President Lyndon Johnson had sent bombing raids and troops to Vietnam in 1964. However, in July 1965 he greatly escalated U.S. involvement in the war when he authorized sending 175,000 to 200,000 troops to the region with a promise of more if necessary. In the following selection, Larry Berman describes the debates that took place among Johnson and his top advisers in the weeks leading up to the decision. He notes that Johnson chose to downplay the magnitude of his troop commitment. This decision to escalate the war, as well as the secrecy that surrounded it, had enormous consequences for both the nation and Johnson's presidency. Berman is a professor of political science at the University of California at Davis and the director of the University's Washington Center. He is the author of *Lyndon Johnson's War: The Road to Stalemate in Vietnam* and *Planning a Tragedy: The Americanization of the War in Vietnam.*

Throughout June and July 1965 the question of Americanizing the war was at the center of all foreign policy discussion. Undersecretary of State George Ball first attempted to influence President Johnson's future ability to control events. In an 18 June memorandum entitled "Keeping the Power of Decision in the South Vietnam Crisis," Ball argued that the

Larry Berman, "Coming to Grips with Lyndon Johnson's War," *Diplomatic History*, vol. 17, 1993, pp. 523–31. Copyright © 1993 by Blackwell Publishers. Reproduced by permission.

United States was on the threshold of a new war. "In raising our commitment from 50,000 to 100,000 or more men and deploying most of the increment in combat roles we were beginning a new war—the United States directly against the Viet Cong. The President's most difficult continuing problem in South Vietnam is to prevent 'things' from getting into the saddle—or, in other words, to keep control of policy and prevent the momentum of events from taking command."

The president needed to understand the effect of losing control: "Perhaps the large-scale introduction of American forces with their concentrated fire power will force Hanoi and the Viet Cong to the decision we are seeking. On the other hand, we may not be able to fight the war successfully enough—even with 500,000 Americans in South Vietnam we must have more evidence than we now have that our troops will not bog down in the jungles and rice paddies—while we slowly blow the country to pieces." Ball tried to review the French experience for Johnson, reminding the president that "the French fought a war in Vietnam, and were finally defeated—after seven years of bloody struggle and when they still had 250,000 combat-hardened veterans in the field, supported by an army of 205,000 South Vietnamese. To be sure, the French were fighting a colonial war while we are fighting to stop aggression. But when we have put enough Americans on the ground in South Vietnam to give the appearance of a white man's war, the distinction as to our ultimate purpose will have less and less practical effect."

Ball urged the president to act cautiously—make a commitment to the one hundred thousand level, but no more. The summer would then be used as a test of U.S. military performance and South Vietnam's resolve. Ball focused on the political context in South Vietnam. "We cannot be sure how far the cancer has infected the whole body politic of South Vietnam and whether we can do more than administer a cobalt treatment to a terminal case." (In a later memorandum Ball wrote "politically, South Vietnam is a lost cause. The country is bled white from twenty years of war and the people are sick of it. . . . Hanoi has a government and a purpose and a discipline. The 'government' in Saigon is a travesty. In a very real sense, South Vietnam is a country with an army and no government. In my view, a deep commitment of United States forces in a land war in South Vietnam would be a catastrophic error. If ever there was an occasion for a tactical withdrawal, this is it.") Ball recommended that the president direct his top advisers to prepare a plan for accelerating the land war, a plan for a vigorous diplomatic offensive designed to bring about a political settlement; and, perhaps most difficult, plans for bringing about a military or political solution—"short of the ultimate U.S. objectives—that can be attained without the substantial further commitment of U.S. forces." Ball recognized that his last proposal should "be regarded as plans for cutting losses and eventually disengaging from an untenable situation."

Robert McNamara's Recommendations

Ball's arguments would have little influence on policymakers. In retrospect there was a remarkable cogency to his position that fell on deaf ears. Ball was isolated from the majority opinion among policymakers, an undersecretary of state taking on the highest ranking officials in government—beginning with the Secretary of Defense, Robert McNamara, and with Ball's own superior, Secretary of State Dean Rusk. On 26 June McNamara circulated his "Program of Expanded Military and Political Moves with Respect to Vietnam." McNamara admitted that the Vietcong were clearly winning the war and that "the tide almost certainly cannot begin to turn in less than a few months and may not for a year or more; the war is one of attrition and will be a long one." McNamara defined winning as the creation of "conditions for a favorable settlement by demonstrating to the VC/DRV [Vietcong/Democratic Republic of (North) Vietnam] that the odds are against their winning. Under present conditions, however, the chances of achieving this objective are small—and the VC are winning now—largely because the ratio of guerrilla to anti-guerrilla forces is unfavorable to the government." Secretary McNamara developed three options for the president: (1) cut U.S. losses and withdraw with the best conditions that could be arranged; (2) continue at about the present level, with U.S. forces limited to about seventy-five thousand, holding on and playing for the breaks while recognizing that the U.S. position would probably grow weaker; (3) expand substantially the U.S. military pressure against the Vietcong in the South and the North Vietnamese in the North. At the same time launch a vigorous effort on the political side to get negotiations started.

McNamara unequivocally supported the third option—a series of expanded military moves as prerequisites for a negotiated settlement on U.S. terms. The secretary recommended that US/GVN [Republic of (South) Vietnam] ground strength be increased to whatever force levels were necessary to show the VC that they "cannot win." The increases would bring U.S. and third-country troop levels to forty-four battalions and be accomplished by a call-up of one hundred thousand reserves. McNamara's military recommendations included a quarantine on the movement of all war supplies into North Vietnam, the mining of North Viet-

Johnson's decision to commit more troops to Vietnam was debated within his administration.

nam's (DRV) harbors, the destruction of all rail and highway bridges from China to Hanoi, armed reconnaissance of communication lines from China, destruction of all war-making supplies inside of North Vietnam, and destruction of all airfields and SAM [surface to air missile] sites.

Conflicting Views

Writing directly to McNamara on 30 June, National Security Adviser McGeorge Bundy criticized the secretary's position, deriding it as "rash to the point of folly." Bundy was critical of tripling the U.S. air effort "when the value of the air action we have taken is sharply disputed." It was also preposterous to consider mining "at a time when nearly everyone agrees the real question is not in Hanoi, but in South Vietnam." Bundy was extremely critical of McNamara's proposed deployment figure, arguing that a 200,000-man level was based "simply on the increasing weakness of Vietnamese forces. But this is a slippery slope toward the U.S. responsibility and corresponding fecklessness on the Vietnamese side." Bundy noted that McNamara's paper "omits examination of the upper limit of U.S. liability." Bundy asked, "If we need 200 thousand men now for these quite limited missions, may we not need 400 thousand later? Is this a rational course of action? Is there any real prospect that U.S. regular forces can conduct the antiguerrilla operations which would probably remain the central problem in South Vietnam?" Bundy concluded with a question: "What is the real object of the exercise? If it is to get to the conference table, what results do we seek there? Still more brutally, do we want to invest 200,000 men to cover an eventual retreat? Can we not do that just as well where we are?"

Assistant Secretary of State William Bundy joined the battle with a memorandum and position paper entitled "A Middle Way Course of Action in South Vietnam." The plan involved moving ahead slowly and testing military capabilities and limits. Bundy believed that his plan avoided the pitfalls of either Ball's or McNamara's alternatives. "It may not give us quite as much chance of a successful outcome as the major military actions proposed in the McNamara memo, but it avoids to a major extent the very serious risks involved in this program in any case, and the far more disastrous outcome that would eventuate if we acted along the lines of the McNamara memo and still lost South Vietnam."

William Bundy's program rejected withdrawal or negotiated concessions and equally rejected a decision to raise U.S. force levels above eighty-five thousand. In Bundy's carefully selected words the program provided "a fair test" because "we simply do not know, and probably cannot know, whether raising the U.S. force level and combat involvement would (1) cause the Vietnamese government and especially the army to let up (2) create adverse public reactions to our whole presence on 'white men' and 'like the French' grounds."

Johnson next heard from Secretary of State Dean Rusk. In a rare personal memorandum to the president on 1 July that had not been circulated to the other principals, Rusk argued that "the central objective of the United States in South Vietnam must be to insure that North Vietnam not succeed in taking over or determining the future of South Vietnam by force, i.e. again defined as denial. We must accomplish this objective without a general war if possible." The war aim of the United States was not and could not be concerned with hypothetical issues such as what the South Vietnamese people would do if left alone: "The sole basis for employing U.S. forces is the aggression from the North." If this aggression were removed, the U.S. forces would also leave. Rusk rejected Ball's position by casting the issue within a much broader context with significant consequences. "There can be no serious debate about the fact that we have a commitment to assist the South Vietnamese to resist aggression from the North. . . . The integrity of the U.S. commitment is the principal pillar of peace throughout the world. If that commitment becomes unreliable, the communist world would draw conclusions that would lead to our ruin and almost certainly to a catastrophic war.". . .

President Johnson now decided to send Secretary McNamara to Vietnam, ostensibly to meet with General Westmoreland and ascertain force requirements. McNamara's trip received much public attention, and the president's public statement hinted at the possibility of major escalation. On the second day of McNamara's visit to Saigon, he received a back channel cable of the utmost importance from his deputy, Cyrus Vance. "Yesterday I met three times with highest authority [President Johnson] on actions associated with 34 battalion plan," the cable read. (The remaining ten battalions of the forty-four-battalion request were to come from Korea and Australia.) Vance went on to summarize what Johnson had told him. (This is perhaps the most significant declassification available to scholars):

1. It is his current intention to proceed with 34 battalion plan.

2. It is impossible for him to submit supplementary budget request of more than $300–$400 million to Congress before next January.

3. If larger request is made to Congress, he believes this will kill domestic legislative program.

4. We should be prepared to explain to the Congress that we have adequate authority and funds, by use of deficit financing, $700 million supplemental [appropriation] and possible small current supplemental to finance recommended operations until next January, when we will be able to come up with clear and precise figures as to what is required.

I asked highest authority whether request for legislation authorizing call-up of reserves and extension of tours of duty would be acceptable in the light of his comments concerning domestic program, and he said that it would.

I pointed out that we would have great difficulties with Senator [John] Stennis concerning this course of action. He said that he recognized that but we would just have to bull it through. He requested that I talk to Senator [Richard] Russell Monday and I will.

Johnson had clearly made his decision to Americanize the war by changing the entire context of commitment. When McNamara returned to Washington on 20 July he presented the president with a report warning of the incipient collapse of South Vietnam. McNamara elaborated and defended an option of "expand[ing] promptly and substantially the US military pressure . . . while launching a vigorous effort on the political side." McNamara called for approval of Westmoreland's request for 100,000 more American troops, which would bring the American troop level up to thirty-four battalions (175,000 troops), or forty-four battalions (200,000) if third-country troops (principally Korean) proved available. He indicated that a twenty-seven-battalion second-phase increase of another 100,000 men might be needed by early 1966, with further increments thereafter. McNamara also urged the president to ask Congress to permit calling up 235,000 reservists to active service and to provide a supplemental appropriation to cover the increased costs of the war.

The McNamara proposal became the focal point of extensive White House deliberations over the next few days. At both the NSC [National Security Council] meeting of 21 July and the Joint Chiefs meeting the following day, Johnson provides ample evidence of his awareness that an upper limit deployment might very well be in the range of six hundred thousand men. At one meeting he asked the Joint Chiefs "do all of you think the Congress and the people will go along with 600,000 people and billions of dollars being spent 10,000 miles away?" The declassified minutes from the meetings of 21 July show that Johnson challenged Ball to prove a case that could not be proven—that the consequences of non-engagement (really disengagement via neutralization) would be better than military engagement. "You have pointed out the danger," President Johnson told Ball, "but you haven't really proposed an alternative course." To illustrate just how intent policymakers had become in molding their local ally during the meeting, Henry Cabot Lodge noted that "there is not a tradition of a national government in Saigon. There are no roots in the country. Not until there is tranquility can you have any stability. I don't think we ought to take this government seriously. There is simply no one who can do anything. We have to do what we think we ought to do regardless of what the Saigon government does. As we move ahead on a new phase, we have the right and the duty to do certain things with or without the government's approval.'

Ball's Final Day in Court

Ball's final day in court came that afternoon when he faced the president and his peers. Ball told the group that

> we cannot win. . . . The war will be long and protracted. The most we can hope for is a messy conclusion. There remains a great danger of intrusion by the Chinese. But the biggest problem is the problem of the long war. The Korean experience was a galling one. The correlation between Korean casualties and public opinion showed support stabilized at 50 percent. As casualties increase, the pressure to strike at the very jugular of North Vietnam will become very great. I am concerned about world opinion. If we could win in a year's time, and win decisively, world opinion would be alright. However, if the war is long and protracted, as I believe it will

be, then we will suffer because the world's greatest power cannot defeat guerrillas.

Reprinted below is part of the dialogue that followed Ball's recommendation:

The President: But George, wouldn't all these countries say that Uncle Sam was a paper tiger, wouldn't we lose credibility breaking the word of three presidents, if we did as you have proposed? It would seem to be an irresponsible blow. But I gather you don't think so?

Ball: No sir. The worse blow would be that the mightiest power on earth is unable to defeat a handful of guerrillas.

The President: Then you are not basically troubled by what the world would say about our pulling out?

Ball: If we were actively helping a country with a stable government, it would be a vastly different story. Western Europeans look upon us as if we got ourselves into an imprudent situation.

McNamara: Ky will fall soon. He is weak. We can't have elections there until there is physical security, and even then there will be no elections because as Cabot said, there is no democratic tradition.

McGeorge Bundy: To accept Ball's argument would be a radical switch in policy without visible evidence that it should be done. George's analysis gives no weight to losses suffered by the other side. The world, the country, and the Vietnamese people would have alarming reactions if we got out.

Rusk: If the communist world found out that the United States would not pursue its commitment to the end, there was no telling where they would stop their expansionism.

Lodge: I feel there is greater threat to start World War III if we don't go in. Can't we see the similarity to our indolence at Munich? I simply can't be as pessimistic as Ball. We have great seaports in Vietnam. We don't need to fight on roads. We have the sea. Let us visualize meeting the VC on our own terms. We don't have to spend all our time in the jungles. If we can secure our bases, the Vietnamese can secure, in time, a political movement to, one, apprehend the terrorists, and two, give intelligence to the government. The procedures for this are known. . . . The Vietnamese have been dealt more casualties than, per capita, we suffered in the Civil War. The Vietnamese soldier is an uncomplaining soldier. He has ideas he will die for.

Meeting with the Joint Chiefs

The following day President Johnson met with the Joint Chiefs to hear their responses to McNamara's program. The chiefs were in a position similar to Ball, in the sense of advocating a policy extreme. The president began the meeting by identifying the three options: "The options open to us are: one, leave the country, with as little loss as possible; two, maintain present force and lose slowly; three, add 100,000 men, recognizing that may not be enough and adding more next year. The disadvantages of number three option are the risk of escalation, casualties high, and the prospect of a long war without victory. I would like you to start out by stating our present position as you see it, and where we can go."

The chiefs warned Johnson that the time had arrived to up the ante, "If we continue the way we are now," warned Admiral D.L. McDonald, "it will be a slow, sure victory for the other side. But putting more men in it will turn the tide and let us know what further we need to do. I wish we had done this long before." When Johnson asked if one hundred thousand men would be enough, McDonald responded that "sooner or later we will force them to the conference table." When Johnson then asked about the chances for success, Paul Nitze answered "if we want to turn the tide, by putting in more men, it would be about sixty-forty." Nitze concluded that another one hundred thousand would be needed by January 1966. When Johnson asked what type of reaction this would produce, General Wheeler noted "since we are not proposing an invasion of the North, the Soviets will step up material and propaganda, and the same with the Chicoms. The North Vietnamese might introduce more regular troops. . . . The one thing all North Vietnam fears is the Chinese. For them to invite Chinese volunteers is to invite China taking over North Vietnam. The weight of judgment is that North Vietnam may reinforce their troops, but they can't match us on a buildup."

The discussion soon turned to the real crux of the matter for LBJ—the costs of escalation and the change in mission. When Admiral McDonald recommended giving Westmoreland all he needed as well as mobilizing the reserves and increasing draft calls, President Johnson asked "do you have any ideas of what this will cost? Do you have any idea what effect this will have on our economy?" Secretary McNamara responded "twelve billion dollars in 1966. It would not require wage and price controls in my judgment. The price index ought not go up more than one point or two." The president asked "doesn't it really mean that if we follow Westmoreland's requests we are in a new war? Isn't this going off the diving board?" Secretary McNamara answered, "if we carry forward all these recommendations, it would be a change in our policy. We have relied on the South to carry the brunt. Now we would be responsible for [a] satisfactory military outcome." President Johnson next heard General Wallace M. Greene report that to accomplish the U.S. objectives it would take "five years, plus 500,000 troops. I think the American people would back you." Johnson asked, "how would you tell the American people what the stakes are." "The place where they will stick by you is the national security stake," responded Greene.

The dialogue was without optimism or short-run terms of reference. President Johnson clearly knew where he was headed when he asked, "do all of you think the Congress and the people will go along with 600,000 people and billions of dollars being spent 10,000 miles away. . . . If you make a commitment to jump off a building and you find out how high it is, you may want to withdraw that commitment." The president's military advisers emphasized that it would take hundreds of thousands of men and several years to achieve military goals. The Joint Chiefs urged Johnson to call up the reserves and the National Guard and to seek public support on national security grounds.

The Announcement

But President Johnson decided that there would be no public announcement of a change in policy. Johnson also rejected McGeorge Bundy's proposal that he go before a joint session of Congress or make his statement in a fireside address. Instead, he simply called a midday press conference. The content as well as the forum of Johnson's message downplayed its significance. The expected call up of the reserves and the request for new funds were absent. Moreover, Johnson also used the afternoon news conference to announce John Chancellor's nomination as head of the United States Information Agency and Abe Fortas's as associate justice of the Supreme Court. JCS [Joint Chiefs of Staff]

Chairman Wheeler cabled General Westmoreland and informed him that McNamara's recommendation for troop increases had been approved and would be announced the next day. "Do not be surprised or disappointed if the public announcement does not set forth the full details of the program, but instead reflects an incremental approach," Wheeler advised. "This tactic will probably be adopted in order to hold down [the] international noise level."

In announcing the troop increase, Johnson did not fully reveal the levels he had now authorized—175,000 to 200,000. Instead, he noted only the immediate force increment—fighting strength would grow from 75,000 to 125,000. Nor did he tell the American people that just a few days earlier Clark Clifford had warned against any substantial buildup of U.S. ground troops. "This could be a quagmire," warned the president's trusted friend. "It could turn into an open-ended commitment on our part that would take more and more ground troops, without a realistic hope of ultimate victory."

Instead, Johnson chose to deceive the American people with respect to the goals of military involvement and their anticipated costs. "Additional forces will be needed later, and they will be sent as requested," LBJ observed at his afternoon press conference. He made a seemingly passing remark that correctly indicated that the American commitment had become open ended: "I have asked the Commanding General, General Westmoreland, what more he needs to meet this mounting aggression. He has told me. We will meet his needs."

The Violent End of Malcolm X

By *Life*

Malcolm X dared to speak out, angrily at times, against the oppression of blacks during a decade that found America struggling with its own conscience. He called on black men and women to ally themselves with the Muslim faith and demand that the long promised "justice for all" be delivered to all of America's citizens. He either excited avid loyalty and intense dislike in the hearts of those who heard him speak. He aroused such a passionate response, be it negative or positive, from the American public that when he was assassinated on February 21, 1965, both the Black Muslims (the organization from which he recently had divorced himself) and the Ku Klux Klan were considered likely suspects. Malcolm X was shot to death while speaking to a predominantly black audience in a Manhattan auditorium. Journalist Gordon Parks, a friend of Malcolm's, witnessed the assassination of the most outspoken and controversial leader of the civil rights movement. In the article from March 1965, Parks recounts Malcolm X's long struggle in the battle for equality, the dramatic events surrounding his violent end, and the outrage of his followers who wanted immediate revenge on the Black Muslims despite the fact that authorities could not tie the shooters to a specific organization.

His life oozing out through a half dozen or more gunshot wounds in his chest, Malcolm X, once the shrillest voice for black supremacy, lay dying on the stage of a

Gordon Parks, "The Violent End of the Man Called Malcolm X," *Life*, March 15, 1965. Copyright © 1965 by Time, Inc. Reproduced by permission.

Manhattan auditorium. Moments before, he had stepped up to the lectern, and 400 of the faithful had settled down expectantly to hear the sort of speech for which he was famous—flaying the hated white man. Then a scuffle broke out in the hall and Malcolm's bodyguards bolted from his side to break it up—only to discover that they had been faked out. At least two men with pistols rose from the audience and pumped bullets into the speaker, while a third cut loose at close range with both barrels of a sawed-off shotgun. In the confusion the pistol men got away. The shotgunner lunged through the crowd and out the door, but not before the guards came to their wits and shot him in the leg. Outside he was swiftly overtaken by other supporters of Malcolm and very likely would have been stomped to death if the police hadn't saved him. Most shocking of all to the residents of Harlem was the fact that Malcolm X had been killed not by "Whitey" but by members of his own race.

The country's Negro community was suddenly faced with the possibility of a fratricidal war. Almost before Malcolm X's body was cold, someone put the torch to the Black Muslims' big Harlem mosque, and Malcolm's dedicated followers served notice that arson alone would not do. Their vendetta was whetted by the memory of Malcolm's predictions. From the time he broke with the Black Muslims a year ago to form his own militant cadre, he had said that Muslim leader Elijah Muhammad was out to get him. Elijah, now the hunted, took refuge in his Chicago headquarters behind a screen of bodyguards, from whence he denied any part in the murder.

Fatalism

Death was surely absent from his face two days before they killed him. He appeared calm and somewhat resplendent with his goatee and astrakhan hat. Much of the old hostility and bitterness seemed to have left him, but the fire and confidence were still there. We talked of those months two years ago when I had traveled with him through the closed world of Muslimism, trying to understand it. I thought back to the austere mosques of the Muslims, the rigidly disciplined elite guard called the Fruit of Islam, the instruction it received in karate, judo and killing police dogs. I recalled the constant vilification of the "white devil," the machinelike obedience of all Muslims, the suspicion and distrust they had for the outsider. But most of all, I remembered Malcolm, sweat beading on his hard-muscled face, his fist slashing the air in front of his audience: "Hell is when you don't have justice! And when you don't have equality, that's hell! And the devil is the one who robs you of your right to be a human being! I don't have to tell you who the devil is. You know who the devil is!" (*"Yes, Brother Malcolm! Tell 'em like it is!"*)

Malcolm said to me now, "That was a bad scene, brother. The sickness and madness of those days—I'm glad to be free of them. It's a time for martyrs now. And if I'm to be one, it will be in the cause of brotherhood. That's the only thing that can save this country. I've learned it the hard way—but I've learned it. And that's the significant thing."

I was struck by the change; and I felt he was sincere, but couldn't his disenchantment with Elijah Muhammad have forced him into another type of opportunism? As recently as December 20 he had yelled at a Harlem rally: "We need a Mau Mau to win freedom and equality in the United States! . . ." There was an inconsistency here. Could he, in his dread of being pushed into obscurity, have trumped up another type of zealotry? I doubted it. He was caught, it seemed, in a new idealism. And, as time bore out, he had given me the essence of what was to have been his brotherhood speech—the one his killers silenced. It was this intentness on brotherhood that cost him his life. For Malcolm, over the objections of his bodyguards, was to rule against anyone being searched before entering the hall that fateful day: "We don't want people feeling uneasy," he said. "We must create an image that makes people feel at home."

Relationship with the Black Muslims

"Is it really true that the Black Muslims are out to get you?" I asked.

"It's as true as we are standing here. They've tried it twice in the last two weeks."

"What about police protection?"

He laughed. "Brother, nobody can protect you from a Muslim but a Muslim—or someone trained in Muslim tactics. I know. I invented many of those tactics."

"Don't you have any protection at all?"

He laughed again. "Oh, there are hunters and there are those who hunt the hunters. But the odds are certainly with those who are most skilled at the game."

He explained that he was now ready to provide a single, unifying platform for all our people, free of political, religious and economic differences. "One big force under one banner," he called it. He was convinced that whatever mistakes he had made after leaving Elijah Muhammad had been in the name of brotherhood. "Now it looks like this brotherhood I wanted so badly has got me in a jam," he said.

Within the last year he had sent me postcards from Saudi Ara-

Malcolm X, one of the most vocal leaders of the civil rights movement, was assassinated in 1965.

bia, Kuwait, Ethiopia, Kenya, Nigeria, Ghana and Tanganyika, and I thanked him for them.

"Everybody's wondering why I've been going back and forth to Africa. Well, first I went to Mecca to get closer to the orthodox religion of Islam. I wanted first-hand views of the African leaders—their problems are inseparable from ours. The cords of bigotry and prejudice here can be cut with the same blade. We have to keep that blade sharp and share it with one another." Now he was sounding like the old Malcolm: "Strangely enough, listening to leaders like Nasser, Ben Bella and Nkrumah awakened me to the dangers of racism. I realized racism isn't just a black and white problem. It's brought blood baths to about every nation on earth at one time or another."

He stopped and remained silent for a few moments. "Brother," he said finally, "remember the time that white college girl came into the restaurant—the one who wanted to help the Muslims and the whites get together—and I told her there wasn't a ghost of a chance and she went away crying?"

"Yes."

"Well, I've lived to regret that incident. In many parts of the African continent I saw white students helping black people. Something like this kills a lot of argument. I did many things as a Muslim that I'm sorry for now. I was a zombie then—like all Muslims—I was hypnotized, pointed in a certain direction and told to march. Well, I guess a man's entitled to make a fool of himself if he's ready to pay the cost. It cost me 12 years."

As we parted he laid his hand on my shoulder, looked into my eyes and said, "A salaam alaikem, brother."

"And may peace be with you, Malcolm," I answered.

Driving home from that last meeting with Malcolm, I realized once more that, despite his extremism and inconsistencies, I liked and admired him. A certain humility was wed to his arrogance. I assumed that his bitterness must have come from his tragic early life. His home in East Lansing, Mich. was burned to the ground by white racists. He had lived for many years with the belief that whites had bludgeoned his father to death and left his body on the tracks to be run over by a streetcar.

Spokesman

Malcolm's years of ranting against the "white devils" helped create the climate of violence that finally killed him, but the private man was not a violent one. He was brilliant, ambitious and honest. And he was fearless. He said what most of us black folk were afraid to say publicly. When he told off "a head-whipping cop"— as he described him—his tongue was coupled with a million other black tongues. When he condemned the bosses of the "rat-infested ghetto," a Harlem full of fervid "amens" could be heard ricocheting off the squalid tenements.

I remember Malcolm's complete devotion to Elijah Muhammad and his words when he was serving as the Muslims' spokesman: "All that Muhammad is trying to do is clean up the mess the white man has made, and the white man should give him credit. He shouldn't run around here calling [Muhammad] a racist and a hate-teacher. White man, call yourself a hate-teacher because you invented hate. Call yourself a racist because you invented the race problem."

Malcolm was not after power in the Muslim organization, but his unquestioning belief in the movement, his personal charm, his remarkable ability to captivate an audience brought him that power. With Elijah aging and ailing, Malcolm became the obvious choice as his successor. But his power and prominence also made him a marked man in the tightly disciplined society. His downfall had started even before his notorious comment on President Kennedy's assassination ("Chickens coming home to roost never did make me sad; they've always made me glad!"). But with that statement he unwittingly made himself more vulnerable.

Family Response

On the night of Malcolm's death, at the home of friends where his family had taken refuge, I sat with his wife Betty, his two oldest children and a group of his stunned followers, watching a television review of his stormy life. When his image appeared on the screen, blasting away at the injustices of "the enemy," a powerfully built man sitting near me said softly, "Tell 'em like it is, Brother Malcolm, tell 'em like it is."

The program ended and Betty got up and walked slowly to the kitchen and stood staring at the wall. Six-year-old Attallah followed and took her mother's hand. "Is Daddy coming back after his speech, Momma?"

Betty put her arms around the child and dropped her head on the refrigerator. "He tried to prepare me for this day," she said. "But I couldn't bring myself to listen. I'd just walk out of the room. The other day—after they tried to bomb us out of the house—was the only time I could stay and listen. I just closed my eyes and hung onto everything he said. I was prepared. That's why I'm ashamed I cried over him when he was lying there all shot up."

Only Qubilah, the four-year-old, seemed to understand that her father wouldn't come again. She tugged at her mother's skirt. "Please don't go out, Momma."

"I won't go, baby. Momma won't go out." She gently pushed the child's head into her lap and told her to go to sleep.

"He was always away," Betty went on, "but I knew he would always come back. We loved each other. He was honest—too honest for his own good, I think sometimes." I started to leave and she said, "I only hope the child I'm carrying is just like his father."

"I hope you get your wish," I said.

Vengeance

I rode back to the city with the heavy-set man who had sat near me during the telecast. He slumped in disgust and guilt. "We could have saved him. We could have saved him," he kept mumbling. "How stupid. How stupid."

"What happens now?" I asked.

"Plenty, brother, plenty. *They* made a mistake. We'll rally now like one big bomb. Those zombies are the biggest obstacle in the progress of our people. They're like quicksand. They swallow up people by the dozens. I got into the organization thinking I was going to help promote progress, and all the stuff they hand you. The next thing I knew, I was hawking their lying newspaper."

"So, what happens now?" I repeated.

"Six brothers are already on their way for the main visit."

"Main visit?"

"There's always been a standing order. If anything happens to Brother Malcolm, six brothers catch the first plane to Chicago, or Phoenix—wherever he's at."

"Elijah Muhammad, you mean?"

"He's the top zombie. He's the first to be visited."

I thought back to the time in Phoenix when I last saw Muhammad and Malcolm together—the two men warmly embracing, their cheeks touching in farewell. I felt empty.

"And after him?" I asked.

"The names on Brother Malcolm's list—the ones who were trying to kill him."

The list, as the newspapers reported, was taken from Malcolm's pocket as he lay dying.

"They know who they are. They've been properly notified," he said solemnly. The list also includes the principal targets for vengeance: the *Muhammad Speaks* newspaper office, the Shabazz Restaurant, Mosque No. 7. "If they're able to hold their meetings at the mosque after tomorrow night," the man said, "I'll join up with them again. Brother, that place will be no more."

I took his word for it—and my despair deepened.

Let Justice Roll Down

By Martin Luther King Jr.

By 1965 substantial gains had been made in the struggle for racial
equality within the United States. After Congress passed the influential
Civil Rights Act of 1964, Martin Luther King Jr. organized a series of
protests designed to help African Americans register to vote, especially
in the deep South. Selma, Alabama, became the focus of these efforts
after some organizers were beaten while demonstrating in the area. In
March 1965 activists and antagonists alike descended on the small
town as King and other members of the movement worked to register
as many African American voters as were eligible to vote. King wrote
the following article for *The Nation* at the same time that events were
unfolding in Selma. However, rather than write specifically about the
movement in Alabama, King discusses the emergence of a "New
South" in which citizens would be united by economic and political
similarities, rather than racial differences. He reviews the recent history
of the civil rights movement and the history of the African American
presence in the South. The article exemplifies King's vision of a well-
planned, skillfully executed civil rights reform.

When 1963 came to a close, more than a few skeptical
voices asked what substantial progress had been
achieved through the demonstrations that had drawn
more than a million Negroes into the streets. By the close of

Martin Luther King Jr., "Let Justice Roll Down," *The Nation*, March 15, 1965, pp. 269–74. Copyright © 1965 by The Nation Magazine/The Nation Company, Inc. Reproduced by permission.

1964, the pessimistic clamor was stilled by the music of major victories. Taken together, the two years marked a historic turning point for the civil rights movement; in the previous century no comparable change for the Negro had occurred. Now, even the most cynical acknowledged that at Birmingham, as at Concord, a shot had been fired that was heard around the world. . . .

After the passage of the Civil Rights Act, and with the defeat of [Republican presidential candidate] Barry Goldwater, there was widespread expectation that barriers would disintegrate with swift inevitability. This easy optimism could not survive the first test. In the hard-core states of the South, while some few were disposed to accommodate, the walls remained erect and reinforced. That was to be expected, for the basic institutions of government, commerce, industry and social patterns in the South all rest upon the embedded institution of segregation. Change is not accomplished by peeling off superficial layers when the causes are rooted deeply in the heart of the organism.

Those who expected a cheap victory in a climate of complacency were shocked into reality by Selma and Marion, Ala. In Selma, the position was implacable resistance. At one point, ten times as many Negroes were in jail as were on the registration rolls. Out of 15,000 eligible to vote, less than 350 were registered.

Selma involves more than disenfranchisement. Its inner texture reveals overt and covert forms of terror and intimidation—that uniquely Southern form of existence for Negroes in which life is a constant state of acute defensiveness and deprivation. Yet if Selma outrages democratic sensibilities, neighboring Wilcox County offers something infinitely worse. Sheriff P.C. Jenkins has held office in Wilcox for twenty-six years. He is a local legend because when he wants a Negro for a crime, he merely sends out word and the Negro comes in to be arrested. This is intimidation and degradation reminiscent only of chattel slavery. This is white supremacist arrogance and Negro servility possible only in an atmosphere where the Negro feels himself so isolated, so hopeless, that he is stripped of all dignity. And as if they were in competition to obliterate the United States Constitution within Alabama's borders, state troopers only a few miles away clubbed and shot Negro demonstrators in Marion.

Are demonstrations of any use, some ask, when resistance is so unyielding? Would the slower processes of legislation and law enforcement ultimately accomplish greater results more painlessly? Demonstrations, experience has shown, are part of the process of stimulating legislation and law enforcement. The federal government reacts to events more quickly when a situation of conflict cries out for its intervention. Beyond this, demonstrations have a creative effect on the social and psychological climate that is not matched by the legislative process. Those who have lived under the corrosive humiliation of daily intimidation are imbued by demonstrations with a sense of courage and dignity that strengthens their personalities. Through demonstrations, Negroes learn that unity and militance have more force than bullets. They find that the bruises of clubs, electric cattle prods and fists hurt less than the scars of submission. And segregationists learn from demonstrations that Negroes who have been taught to fear can also be taught to be fearless. Finally, the millions of Americans on the side lines learn that inhumanity wears an official badge and wields the power of law in large areas of the democratic nation of their pride.

In addition to these ethical and psychological considerations, our work in the black-belt counties of Alabama has enabled us to develop further a tactical pattern whose roots extend back to Birmingham and Montgomery. Our movement has from the earliest days of SCLC [Southern Christian Leadership Conference] adhered to a method which uses nonviolence in a special fashion. We have consistently operated on the basis of total community involvement. It is manifestly easier to initiate actions with a handful of dedicated supporters, but we have sought to make activists of all our people, rather than draw some activists from the mass.

Our militant elements were used, not as small striking detachments, but to organize. Through them, and by patient effort, we have attempted to involve Negroes from industry, the land, the home, the professions; Negroes of advanced age, middle age, youth and the very young. In Birmingham, Montgomery, Selma, St. Augustine and elsewhere, when we marched it was as a community, not as a small and unimpressive, if symbolic, assemblage. The charge that we were outside agitators, devoid of support from contented local Negroes, could not be convincing when the procession of familiar local faces could be seen block after block in solid array.

The second element in our tactics after Montgomery was to formulate demands that covered varied aspects of Negro life. If voting campaigns or lunch-counter sit-ins appeared central in press reports, they were but a part of our broader aims. In Birmingham, employment opportunities was a demand pressed as forcefully as desegregation of public facilities. In Selma, our four points encompass voting rights, employment opportunities, improved interracial communication and paved streets in the Negro neighborhoods. The last demand may appear to Northerners to lack some of the historic importance of voting rights. To the Southern Negro the fact that anyone can identify where the ghetto begins by noting where the pavement ends is one of the many offensive experiences in his life. The neighborhood is degraded to degrade the person in it.

We have found that when we make a package of our demands, our goals are clarified and victory becomes easier. This has not meant that we would refuse to recognize partial gains or to call a pause when we had made significant progress. Taking a leaf from the trade unions, we have accepted less than full victory, knowing that a degree of success is a foundation from which later struggles can be launched for additional gains.

We have come to believe that the combining of concrete demands, flexibly handled, with mass community involvement, all conducted with nonviolent direct action is the formula for ac-

King organized many protests designed to help African Americans gain equality.

complishment in the South. The widespread public interest and sympathy we receive are less a tribute to outstanding personalities than a response to the deeper attraction of a whole people on the move for realizable objectives.

Some may wonder whether the continued turmoil in 1965 implies that the gains of 1963–64 were illusory. Not so. We have already scored victories in the black belt which would have seemed foolish dreams a few years back. Violence has been controlled, though not eliminated. . . .

The fusing of economic measures with civil rights needs; the boldness to penetrate every region of the Old South; the undergirding of the whole by the massive Negro vote, both North and South, all place the freedom struggle on a new elevated level.

The old tasks of awakening the Negro to motion while educating America to the miseries of Negro poverty and humiliation in their manifold forms have substantially been accomplished. Demonstrations may be limited in the future, but contrary to some belief, they will not be abandoned. Demonstrations educate the onlooker as well as the participant, and education requires repetition. That is one reason why they have not outlived their usefulness. Furthermore, it would be false optimism to expect ready compliance to the new law everywhere. The Negro's weapon of nonviolent direct action is his only serviceable tool against injustice. He may be willing to sheath that sword but he has learned the wisdom of keeping it sharp.

The Future of the Movement

Yet new times call for new policies. Negro leadership, long attuned to agitation, must now perfect the art of organization. The movement needs stable and responsible institutions in the communities to utilize the new strength of Negroes in altering social customs. In their furious combat to level walls of segregation and discrimination, Negroes gave primary emphasis to their deprivation of dignity and personality. Having gained a measure of success they are now revealed to be clothed, by comparison with other Americans, in rags. They are housed in decaying ghettos and provided with a ghetto education to eke out a ghetto life. Thus, they are automatically enlisted in the war on poverty as the most eligible combatants. Only when they are in full possession of their civil rights everywhere, and afforded equal economic opportunity, will the haunting race question finally be laid to rest.

What are the key guides to the future? It would not be overoptimistic to eliminate one of the vain hopes of the segregationists—the white backlash. It had a certain reality in 1964, but far less than the segregationists needed. For the most part it was powered by petulance rather than principle. Therefore, when the American people saw before them a clear choice between a future of progress with racial justice or stagnation with ancient privilege, they voted in landslide proportions for justice. President Johnson made a creative contribution by declining to mute this issue in the campaign.

The election of President Johnson, whatever else it might have been, was also an alliance of Negro and white for common interests. Perceptive Negro leadership understands that each of the major accomplishments in 1964 was the product of Negro militancy *on a level that could mobilize and maintain white support.* Negroes acting alone and in a hostile posture toward all whites will do nothing more than demonstrate that their conditions of life are unendurable, and that they are unbearably angry. But this has already been widely dramatized. On the other hand, whites who insist upon exclusively determining the time schedule of change will also fail, however wise and generous they feel themselves to be. A genuine Negro-white unity is the tactical foundation upon which past and future progress depends. . . .

Keep Moving Forward

The fluidity and instability of American public opinion on questions of social change is very marked. There would have been no civil rights progress, nor a nuclear test–ban treaty, without resolute Presidential leadership. The issues which must be decided are momentous. The contest is not tranquil and relaxed. The search for a consensus will tend to become a quest for the least common denominator of change. In an atmosphere devoid of urgency the American people can easily be stupified into accepting slow reform, which in practice would be inadequate reform. "Let Justice roll down like waters in a mighty stream," said the Prophet Amos. He was seeking not consensus but the cleansing action of revolutionary change. America has made progress toward freedom, but measured against the goal the road ahead is still long and hard. This could be the worst possible moment for slowing down. . . .

The contemporary civil rights movement . . . must select from the multitude of issues those principal creative reforms which will have broad transforming power to affect the whole movement of society. Behind these goals it must then tirelessly organize widespread struggle. The specific selection of the correct and appropriate programs requires considerable discussion and is beyond the purview of this study. A few guidelines are, however, immediately evident.

One point of central importance for this period is that the distribution of Negroes geographically makes a single national tactical program impractical. During the Civil War, Frederick Douglass perceived the difference in problems of Negroes in the North and in the South. He championed emancipation, aside from its moral imperatives, because its impact would transform the South. For the North, his principal demand was integration of Negroes into the Union Army.

Similarly today, the Negro of the South requires in the first place the opportunity to exercise elementary rights and to be shielded from terror and oppression by reliable, alert government protection. He should not have to stake his life, his home or his security merely to enjoy the right to vote. On the other hand, in the North, he already has many basic rights and a fair measure of state protection. There, his quest is toward a more significant participation in government, and the restructuring of his economic life to end ghetto existence.

Very different tactics will be required to achieve these disparate goals. Many of the mistakes made by Northern movements may be traced to the application of tactics that work in Birmingham but produce no results in Northern ghettos. Demonstrations in the streets of the South reveal the cruel fascism underlacing the social order there. No such result attends a similar effort in the North. However, rent strikes, school boycotts, electoral alliances summon substantial support from Negroes, and dramatize the specific grievances peculiar to those communities.

With the maturation of the civil rights movement, growing out of the struggles of 1963 and 1964, new tactical devices will emerge. The most important single imperative is that we continue moving forward with the indomitable spirit of those two turbulent years. It is worth recalling the admonition of Napoleon (he was thinking of conquest, but what he said was true also of constructive movements): "In order to have good soldiers, a nation must always be at war."

Peacekeeping in Santo Domingo

By James F. Fixx

News of the Vietnam War permeated the American conscience in 1965. However, the conflict in Vietnam was not the only theater of war for American troops. Just before Easter, a violent uprising became a full-scale civil war in the streets and cities of the Dominican Republic. At first, the civil war was believed to be a battle between Communist insurgents and the existing republic. Following the vigorous anti-Communist precedent established by the U.S. presence in Vietnam, President Lyndon B. Johnson deployed U.S. troops on a peacekeeping mission to the Dominican Republic. Many Dominicans were incensed by the U.S. presence, and rebel forces attempted to convince the United States that they were not Communists.

War correspondent James F. Fixx traveled to Santo Domingo, the capital city of the Dominican Republic, to cover the uprising and to write about the success of the U.S. arbitration efforts. While in Santo Domingo, Fixx followed Peace Corps director Lowell Robert Satin into some of the most dangerous streets and neighborhoods of the war-torn city. Fixx found a city divided between two governments struggling for control of the capital and the country, but he also found that fighters on both sides of the war wanted to settle the matter for themselves without U.S. assistance.

One sweltering afternoon during a lull in the fighting here, I accompanied several hundred rebels, armed and unarmed, who gathered at El Conde Gate in Independence Park for a demonstration. Earlier in the day a top rebel leader had assured U.S. newsmen that, despite reports to the contrary, they were free to enter the city's rebel zone. Although somewhat uneasy at finding myself deep in the stronghold of one of the warring camps, I couldn't help noticing the incongruities of the setting. Atop a building facing the park, a giant billboard advertising Presidente beer overlooked hibiscus bushes bright with blossoms, tangles of lush bougainvillea vines, and an eternal flame that burns here in memory of the nation's patriots. But the billboard also overlooked jeeps bristling with weapons, tanks that had ground their imprint into the grass, and haggard, serious-faced men with rifles and submachine guns and hand grenades slung over their shoulders. As I arrived at the park and made my way into the crowd, a group was rhythmically chanting "Yankee go home!" When I passed them, however, one of their number smiled and clapped me warmly on the back, as if to make it clear that it was only the U.S. troops they were talking about. Meanwhile, moving among the crowd selling copies of a hastily assembled rebel newspaper called *Patria: Vocero de la Dominicanidad* was a youth in a soiled, sweaty T-shirt. On the shirt was a picture of the Beatles.

Yankee Go Home

But if one was startled or amused by the contrasts, it soon became apparent that the mood of the gathering was deadly serious. The rebels had sustained heavy casualties. In the northern part of the city they were being steadily squeezed into an increasingly smaller pocket, their backs pressed uncomfortably against the Ozama River, which curls like a muddy ribbon through Santo Domingo. And their movement, which purportedly had begun as a popular effort to restore democratic government, was—or so they insisted—being snagged and sabotaged by 20,000 U.S. troops who, although theoretically neutral, were aiding the rebels' antagonists, the loyalists.

A young man in a blue sports shirt open at the neck mounted the speaker's platform, grasped a microphone, and began to demand loudly that the *Yanquis* go home.

There were cheers from the crowd.

"This is *our* problem," he said, "not the problem of the U.S. Marines."

More cheers.

Then his argument shifted. Punctuating the words with his arms, he shouted: "We must join with the people of Venezuela, with the people of Cuba!"

An angry murmur began to ripple through the crowd, and someone near me said in quiet horror: "A Communist!" Hands reached up to pull the speaker from the platform. He resisted, gripping the microphone. The wire was yanked from its base. He continued to speak, gesticulating at the crowd with the dead microphone. Finally he was pulled from the platform, but he managed to remount it. A rebel aimed an M-1 rifle into the air and fired a shot. A second rebel, standing nearby, answered with two or three shots, and the crowd, myself very much included, fled for cover. The rebels had effectively deprived the unwanted speaker of his audience.

We Are Not Communists

As I crouched behind a parked car, a young rebel took me by the arm and smiled reassuringly. I realized the shooting was now over. The rebel Minister of the Armed Forces was mounting the platform, the crowd was calmer, and I began to move closer in order to hear what he was saying. But I was immediately stopped by a dozen or so rebels who surrounded me, pleading with me to understand that the first speaker had in no way represented their views.

"We are not Communists," they said. "How can we make the Americans understand that we are not Communists?"

They explained that, certainly, radical opportunists had joined their movement—no one would deny that—but the movement itself, they said, was anti-Communist and democratic. They were bitter at the presence of the apparently Communist speaker, and they were disappointed and frustrated that his speech had been witnessed by a *Norteamericano*. The Minister of the Armed Forces clearly echoed their convictions when he said, "This war is not a problem for any other country. It is a problem for the Dominican Republic."

The incident reflected the focal issue in the U.S. presence in this city. It was fear of a Communist takeover that helped trigger President Johnson's decision to send troops to Santo Domingo

("The American nations," he had said, "cannot, must not, and will not permit the establishment of another Communist government in the Western Hemisphere"). It was subsequent doubt about the degree of Communist involvement in the revolution that produced the U.S.'s agonizing soul-searching and shifts of position. And it was the combination of both that, in the opinion of many observers here, may in the end have given substantial comfort to the Communists by touching off an explosion of anti-Americanism.

Whatever the political causes and complexities of the war, however, it is immediately apparent to a visitor that its effects are the grimly familiar ones of war anywhere. Just before the May 21 cease-fire, I drove through scattered gunfire in the loyalist-held areas in the northern part of the city, which only the day before had been in rebel hands. Here, houses had been pocked by bullets, garbage littered the streets, and cars had been overturned to form barricades. At one house, a child accepted a banana and remarked that she had eaten nothing but occasional scraps for three weeks. At another, a pregnant woman lay weakly on a cot, a shrapnel wound in her lower leg; she had had no medical treatment since a shell exploded in her backyard the day before. And at still another house in the same neighborhood, a man reported that the family next door had fled in terror after their baby had been struck by shrapnel and killed. The recent death toll, after heavy fighting in crowded residential districts, was estimated at more than 100, and since the struggle began an estimated 2,000 people had died (among them eighteen U.S. servicemen).

Even at the far western end of the city, some two miles from most of the fighting, the signs of war are inescapable. In front of the vast Hotel Embajador, built as a tourist showplace by dictator Rafael Leonidas Trujillo Molina, six 105-millimeter howitzers have been set solidly into earth-and-sandbag bunkers, and coveys of helicopters clatter into the air from the golf course nearby. In the rear patio of the hotel, facing the Caribbean, the free-form swimming pool is unused except as a storage tank for the troops' water supply, and the circular bar at the pool's edge, sheltered by a quaintly tropical thatched roof, is deserted. The lobby and corridors of the Embajador swarm endlessly with diplomatic personnel and newsmen, all of whom carry candles at night because electrical power is more likely to be off than on. The carpets are thick with mud, and refugees awaiting evacuation, both children and adults, sleep each night on the couches and chairs in the lobby. An unmistakably anxious atmosphere prevailed here at the height of the struggle, especially after rebels landed two mortar rounds near enough to jar windowpanes.

The Revolution Begins

The chaos began to envelop Santo Domingo on Saturday, April 24. Early that afternoon, the rebels, or constitutionalists, notified a local radio station of their rebellion and the news was broadcast. Dominicans, jubilant at the thought of upsetting the junta government of Donald Reid Cabral, which had come to power after the overthrow of the popular President Juan D. Bosch in September 1963, crowded the streets in celebration, honking automobile horns and chanting "Bosch! Bosch! Viva Bosch!" Here, they hoped, was their opportunity to escape from the hardships of the Reid regime. Unemployment was chronic, government workers had received no pay in five months, and there was a vexing catalogue of other annoyances, minor and major. But the joy was short-lived. Within moments Radio Santo Domingo, the government station, was denying that any coup had taken place. Quiet returned to the city for about an hour as the denials continued. Finally, however, listeners heard people shouting in the studio, followed by a voice saying, "The government of Reid Cabral has fallen! Get into the streets and celebrate! Viva Bosch!" Loyalist troops later retook Radio Santo Domingo, but it was too late to save the Reid government. The rebels, although split into several factions, had by that time gathered a momentum that could not be stopped. Two days later some 3,000 weapons were distributed to them at Independence Park, and on May 4 a so-called constitutional president was elected. He was a stocky, thirty-two-year-old army colonel named Francisco Caamaño Denó, who—ironically, in view of the fact that he would soon spend much of his time fighting U.S. Marines—had in 1954 received amphibious training with the U.S. Marines in California and had the following year taken an officers' course at the Quantico, Virginia, Marine base. Colonel Caamaño's followers proudly proclaimed him legitimate successor to Mr. Bosch, the government's last freely elected president.

   The revolution was in full swing by the time the weapons had been distributed, and Santo Domingo's normal life collapsed. Early Tuesday morning, U.S. citizens were instructed by the embassy to meet at the Embajador Hotel if they wished to be evacuated to safety. When the nearly 1,000 Americans who had decided to evacuate arrived, they were horrified to find the hotel in rebel hands. It was what happened next, Ambassador William Tapley Bennett, Jr., said later, that was a major factor in the decision to call in the Marines. At about 8:30 that morning, according to witnesses, twenty-five armed rebels arrived at the hotel and ordered the Americans to lie face-down on the grass. For no apparent reason, they peppered the outside of the building with machine-gun fire, herded the terrified evacuees into the hotel lobby, and again fired round after senseless round. Miraculously, no one was injured. But hours later, on orders from President Johnson, the first contingent of Marines—400 of them—arrived in Santo Domingo.

Gunboat Diplomacy

It was the beginning of a massive buildup of U.S. troops that eventually brought the total in the area to 32,800 (including some 10,000 men aboard Navy vessels just offshore). It was also the beginning of charges of "gunboat diplomacy," of using, as one diplomat put it, a cannon to kill a fly, and of violation of the Organization of the American States (OAS) charter (specifically, critics cited the provision that says, "No state or group of states has the right to intervene directly or indirectly for any reason whatever in the internal or external affairs of any other state").

But President Johnson, with Castro's takeover of Cuba still painfully fresh in his mind, felt he had justification for acting as he did, and he tried to make that justification clear. A list of fifty-three "known and active Communists," alleged to be part of Colonel Caamaño's rebel movement, was made public, and the President left no doubt that he would not tolerate another Cuba in this hemisphere. Unquestionably he anticipated heavy criticism, but in his mind and the minds of his advisers criticism was apparently preferable to the creation of yet another Communist state.

The events that followed are by this time well known. With U.S. backing, a civilian-military counterrevolutionary junta was established under the leadership of Brigadier General Antonio Imbert Barreras, one of the men who four years ago assassinated Rafael Trujillo and thereby became something of a national hero. Despite professions of U.S. neutrality, the loyalists received financial aid and military support in their struggle to halt the rebels. There was, in fact, no doubt in the minds of observers here that

American military power was squarely on the side of the loyalists. G.I.'s routinely referred to loyalist troops as "friendlies" and to rebels as "unfriendlies." And on the very day that I heard Deputy Secretary of Defense Cyrus R. Vance describe allegations of U.S. partiality as categorically false, I asked a young Marine why he thought he had been sent to Santo Domingo. His answer came without an instant's hesitation: "To kill the goddam rebels."

The Marines Land

The Marines, having landed in force by early May, proceeded to carve out a narrow supply corridor through rebel-held territory in the downtown area west of the Ozama River and to create an "international safety zone" by clearing snipers from one part of the city. The corridor provided a relatively safe passageway to San Isidro air base, in open country ten miles east of Santo Domingo, but it also had the effect of dividing the rebel troops in the northern and southern parts of the city and of bottling them up in strategically cramped positions. Armed rebels could pass from one area to the other, it was reported, only through sewers, while the junta troops were allowed much freer movement.

As U.S. troops became more and more solidly enmeshed in the Dominican war, officials began to find it increasingly difficult to fit the rebel movement into the Cuban pattern. It was becoming clear that, although Communists undoubtedly had joined the movement after it began, the movement itself was probably not specifically Communist. (I was present at rebel headquarters in the downtown Edificio Copello one day when Colonel Caamaño said sadly, "I believe the Americans were misinformed by Ambassador Bennett." He added that he was anxious for peace but was adamant about a return to the 1963 democratic constitution.) The suspicion began to grow that the revolution may in fact have been a popular movement that had resulted largely from the cruel heritage of Trujillo's thirty-one years in power—a harsh era that had left the country fractured by hatreds, lacking in seasoned moderate leadership, and with practically no democratic experience or machinery. More and more Dominicans began to admit publicly that they sympathized with the rebel cause, and even some U.S. officials warily conceded that the rebels probably had the support of a vast majority of the people.

It was late May when U.S. policy finally began to reflect the change. Officials seemed increasingly embarrassed by the Imbert junta it had helped create, particularly when General Imbert violated an OAS-negotiated cease-fire and stubbornly boasted, "I will fight even if the Marines are turned against me." White House adviser McGeorge Bundy was dispatched to Santo Domingo to help establish a moderate government acceptable both to the rebels and the loyalists, and even Colonel Caamaño, who had earlier complained bitterly about U.S. partiality to the loyalists, said he had observed a welcome change in the U.S. position. He was now convinced, he said, that "President Johnson wants the American forces neutral."

Even though U.S. policy had by this time apparently come almost full circle, it was much too late to head off the searing criticism that was being directed at the Marines, at the government, and at the embassy. Earlier in the month former President Bosch had called the U.S. action just as immoral as the Soviet repression of the 1956 Hungarian revolt, insisting that the constitutionalist rebels would have won at the outset if U.S. troops had not intervened (there is a widespread conviction here that the U.S. action unquestionably prolonged the war and contributed to the bloodshed). The U.S. was accused of having succumbed to "a wave of anti-Communist panic . . . at a moment when the President desperately needed sober counsel" and of "exaggerated . . . zeal in meeting the Dominican crisis." In London the *Times* remarked that "The U.S. is doing its best to appear as if it has reverted to the American colonialism of the nineteenth century," and the *New Statesman*, comparing the U.S. action in Santo Domingo to the earlier Soviet action in Hungary, asked, "Why should the Americans escape international opprobrium if the Russians were rightly condemned before world opinion?"

Unanswered Questions

Whatever the precise validity of such criticism, it is now clear that at the very least the Dominican action has raised some sober questions.

Why, for example, were the President's initial intelligence reports about the revolution apparently at odds with the facts? Early in April, Ambassador Bennett had sent a note to Thomas C. Mann, Under Secretary of State for Economic Affairs, saying in part: "Little foxes, some of them red, are chewing at the grapes. . . . A diminution of our effort or failure to act will result in a bitter wine." Was excessive emphasis put on the presence of

Communists in the Dominican Republic?

Why, as one Dominican asked me, did it require 30,000 U.S. troops to cope with fifty-three Communists? Had the massive military force been adequately weighed against the grave erosion of good will that would inevitably result from the first such Caribbean intervention in a generation?

Was violation of the OAS charter justified by the circumstances? A month after the revolution began, it is true, an OAS peace-keeping force was finally being formed, but it was already too late, in the minds of most Latin Americans, to erase the damage done by the unilateral intervention.

Why was such a haze of misinformation released by the U.S. Embassy in Santo Domingo? On April 28, to cite one example, Ambassador Bennett told newsmen about alleged rebel atrocities and related how Colonel Juan Calderon, among others, had been machine-gunned to death by Colonel Caamaño himself. Two weeks later Colonel Calderon was released from a military hospital, recovered from a bullet wound received in a skirmish at the National Palace. And Lowell Robert Satin, thirty-three-year-old director of the Peace Corps in the Dominican Republic, who at various times personally retrieved a total of eight Marine prisoners from the rebels, informed me that, despite all the atrocity stories, every one of them had been well treated by their captors.

Why, finally, did the U.S. apparently find it impossible, well before the Dominican revolution began, to distinguish between the legitimate aspirations of a people eager to better their condition and the aims of the Communists who would inevitably flock to the scene of any unrest? An American who lives and works in the Dominican Republic commented bitterly one day, "This war has an economic, a social, and a political aspect, and, my God, we're on the wrong side of all three."

The Lessons

What are the lessons of the Dominican revolution? What can be salvaged from the diplomatic wreckage?

Perhaps valuable momentum has now been created for formation of a permanent standby peace-keeping force that would obviate the necessity (and the temptation) for unilateral action by any nation in the hemisphere. The OAS force in Santo Domingo, the first in the organization's seventeen-year history, will almost certainly have to remain for many months as a counterbalance to the country's political confusion, and the precedent may serve a constructive purpose.

Perhaps Washington will take greater pains to gather accurate intelligence on political conditions in the hemisphere and will evaluate it more cautiously. President Johnson proved in the Dominican crisis that he can ask the right questions and change his mind swiftly if need be. Perhaps next time he will be able to ask the questions—and get the answers—in time.

Perhaps, too, the Dominican incident will strengthen the fine art of making distinctions—the distinction between Castro's Cuba and the rest of Latin America, between a popular democratic revolution and a Communist revolution, between our own nation's commitment to democratic procedures and the methods of totalitarianism.

As one Latin American said here the other day, "It would be a sad thing if the United States, a nation that was born in revolution, would not allow another nation the same privilege."

The Plight of the Unseen Farmer

By Truman Moore

Perhaps the plight of the migrant farmers of the United States would have gone unnoticed and largely forgotten if not for the roiling social fervor of the 1960s. In 1965 the devastation of the Great Depression was twenty-five years past and most Americans assumed that the long migrations of homeless and transient farmworkers had also passed. However, the strikes that began in 1965 in the grape fields of California disclosed the existence of a nomadic nation of workers who hauled their families from farm to farm looking for work and food.

Writer Truman Moore spent much of the early sixties trailing the scores of migrant workers who seemed to pass unseen in and out of the great farmlands of the United States. Though 1965 was the year in which many voices clamored for justice, these farmers were part of a group that, because of circumstance, was unable to speak for itself. Along with other activists who sought to improve the status of itinerant workers in the country, Moore published a book detailing the bleak lives, poor wages, and shoddy living conditions of the men, women, and children who worked to make America the land of plenty.

Each year when the harvest begins, thousands of buses haul thousands of crews to fields across America as millions of migrant workers hit the road. They ride in flatbed trucks or old condemned school buses patched together for just one more season. They go by car: Hudson bombers with engines knocking, laying a smoke screen of oil; pre-war Fords packed with bags, bundles, pots and pans, children crying. They go in pickups made into mobile tents—a home for the season. They ride the rods of the "friendly" Southern Pacific.

They come from farms in the Black Belt, from closed mines in the mountains of Kentucky and West Virginia, from wherever men are desperate for work. They come by whatever means they can find. These are the migrants—the gasoline gypsies, the rubber tramps—crossing and recrossing America, scouring the countryside in a land where the season never ends. There's always a harvest somewhere.

From Florida to Oregon the fruit tramp pursues the orchards. From Texas to Michigan the berry migrants work from field to field. Two million men, women, and children invade every state of the Union to pick fruit, to chop cotton, to scrap beans, to top onions, to bunch carrots, to pull corn, to fill their hampers with the richest harvest earth ever yielded to man. . . .

Migrant Living Conditions

Across America there are tens of thousands of migrant camps. They are in the valleys and in the fields, on the edges of cities and towns. Some are half deserted. Some are behind barbed wire and even patrolled by armed guards. Migrant camps are within commuting distance of Times Square, under the vapor trails of Cape Kennedy, and surrounded by missile sites in the Southwest. They have names like Tin Top, Tin Town, Black Cat Row, Cardboard City, Mexico City, The Bottoms, Osceola (for whites), Okeechobee (for blacks), and Griffings Path.

Negroes from the Black Belt are dismayed by camps they find up North. Okies and Arkies who migrate today find camps much like those the Joads found in [John Steinbeck's novel] *The Grapes of Wrath*. You can drive from New York to California and never see a migrant camp. You have to know where to look. To borrow a popular analogy, a tar-paper curtain separates the migrants from the rest of America.

Let us look at a typical migrant camp which we will call Shacktown. Shacktown is owned by a corporate farm, one of whose foremen is in charge of the camp. "But mostly," he says, "we just turn it over to the people to run for themselves." In other words, no one collects garbage or maintains the camp in any way. The camp is built on the grower's sprawling farm. It cannot be reached without trespassing, and several signs along the road remind the visitor of this fact. Even finding it is difficult. Local residents are suspicious of outsiders who are interested in migrant camps. Requests for directions are met with icy stares.

Shacktown was built about fifteen years ago. No repairs to speak of have been made since then. Most of the screen doors are gone. The floors sag. The roofs leak. The Johnsons, a Shacktown family, have a six-month-old baby and five older children. "When it rains," says Mr. Johnson, "it leaks on our bed and all over the room. At night when it rains, we have to stand up with the baby so he don't get wet and catch pneumonia."

All the rooms in Shacktown are the same size, eight feet by sixteen. When the Johnsons moved in, they found they needed much more space. They sawed through the wall, a single thickness of one by six inch pine, and made a door to the next cabin, which was not occupied. The exterior walls are unpainted and uninsulated. They keep out neither wind nor rain, sight nor sound. Cracks between the boards are big enough to put your hand through. There is no privacy, and the Johnsons, like most Shacktown families, have learned to live without it. The windows are simple cutouts with a hatch propped open from the bottom. Some have a piece of clothlike screening tacked on.

The only touch of the twentieth century in the Johnsons' cabin is a drop cord that hangs down from the ceiling. It burns a single light bulb, plays a small worn radio, and when it works, an ancient television set that Mr. Johnson bought for ten dollars, through which they get their only glimpse of urban, affluent America.

Although there are trees nearby, the camp is built on a barren red-clay hill, baked by a blazing summer sun. There are four barrack-type frame buildings, divided into single rooms. Behind the barracks are two privies, both four-seaters. The door to the women's privy is missing, but the rank growth of weeds serves as a screen. There are no lights, and no one uses the toilets after dark. The Johnsons use a slop jar at night. It is kept in the kitchen and used for garbage, too.

There is virtually no hope of keeping out the flies that swarm around the privies. . . .

Water and Health Problems

For most of the year the cabins are miserably hot. Refrigeration is nonexistent, and perishable foods seldom find their way to the migrant's table. The baby's milk sours quickly, and he is given warm Coke. Good water is always scarce in Shacktown. Between the long buildings there is a single cold-water tap. The faucet leaks, and there is no drainage. A small pond has developed, and the faucet is reached by a footbridge made of boards propped on rocks. This is the only water in camp.

Just keeping clean is a struggle. Water must be carried in from the spigot, heated over the kerosene stove, and poured into the washtub. In the evening, the oldest children are sent out with buckets to stand in line for water. Sometimes when the line is too long, the Johnsons buy their water from a water dealer, who sells it by the bucket. "We get some of our water down the road about five miles," says Mrs. Johnson. "Sometimes I get so tired I'd just like to go in and die. We have to boil the water and then take it to the tub to wash the clothes. We have to boil water for washing dishes. The last camp we was in had a shower, but you had to stand in line for it half a day, especially in the summer."

The problem of getting water is widespread in migrant camps. A Mexican national in California said his camp was without water for a week. "The contractor said the pump broke. There was a small rusty pipe that brought enough water for washing the hands and the face, but we could not wash our clothes, and we could not take a bath for a week. The inspector ordered the pump be fixed right away. Now the water from the baths is pumped out of a big hole, and it flows through a ditch between the bunkhouse and the tents. When it makes warm weather it smells very bad. To me it looks like the contractor is not afraid of the inspector."

When several children in a Swansboro, North Carolina, camp became ill, a young minister named Jack Mansfield had the water in the camp tested. It was found to be contaminated. He reported this to the county health office, but they said nothing could be done since the camp had been condemned long ago. . . .

Sanitary Conditions

As bad as conditions are in the camps where the migrants live, they are worse in the fields where they work. A Florida Health Department report noted that at times crews refused to harvest fields because of the human waste deposited there by an earlier crew. . . .

The fields of the modern factory farm are immense. And there are no bathrooms. A Catholic priest observed that "most consumers would gag on their salad if they saw these conditions, the lack of sanitary conditions, under which these products are grown and processed."

After a tour of leading farm states, Senator Harrison Williams of New Jersey said: "In the fields . . . sanitation facilities are a rarity. Unlike other sectors of our commerce, agriculture generally does not provide migrant farm workers with field-sanitation facilities such as toilets, hand-washing facilities, and potable drinking water.

"We as consumers have good reason to be uneasy about this situation. Much of our soft food and other products are picked, and often field packed, by migratory farm workers. If we object to filth anywhere, we certainly should object to it in any part of the process that brings the food from the fields to our tables."

One grower, a woman, docked the workers an hour's pay if they left the field to go to the bathroom. The woman stayed with the crew most of the day. The men had to relieve themselves in front of her. They found this humiliating but were unwilling to lose the wage.

Antonio Velez, a field worker in the San Joaquin Valley, said he was told by the grower to drive a pickup truck into the fields which carried two chemical toilets. The grower told him to drive fast so that the toilets would slosh around and be dirty, and no one would want to use them. He was afraid the workers "would lose too much time going to the bathroom." The idea of providing field workers with toilets and clean water strikes most growers as an unnecessary refinement. Consumers who realize that diseases such as amebic dysentery, polio, and infectious hepatitis (to name only a few) can be transmitted through human excreta may not be so convinced of the frivolity of field sanitation. . . .

Migrant Children

The man put down his hamper. "It sure looks like rain," he said. The skies were a bright crystal blue, with only a trace of clouds to the east. The crew kept working, but a few looked up and saw the three men coming down the row. One was the grower, who seldom came around. The other was the crew leader. The third man was a stranger. He carried a brown leather case and a clipboard. The men just nodded as they passed.

They went up and down the rows, the first two walking easily. The third man, the stranger, stumbled now and then—a city man used to flat sidewalks. They crossed the red-clay road and went into the south field. A woman looked up as they came past the stacks of empty crates. Before they were close enough to hear, she turned to the busy crew. "Sure looks like rain." Two small pickers dropped their boxes and darted through the vines and ran into the woods. Someone on the next row passed the word. "Sure looks like rain." Two more children ducked into the vines and ran.

The children hid beyond the road in a small clearing in a clump of scrub oaks. From here they could see the man leave. It was their favorite game. Hiding from the inspector was about the only thing that broke up the long hours in the field. In the camp they played hide and seek this way. When you were "it" you were the inspector. But it was more fun when there was a real inspector.

Luis at twelve was the oldest of the children. He had been to school off and on since he was six, but he was only in the fourth grade. If he ever went back he would be in the fifth grade, because he was older and bigger now. But Luis didn't want to go back. He wanted to run away. He had been around the country a lot. Last year his family went to California and Oregon. One year they went to Arkansas. Once long ago—he was too young to remember when—his father took them to Florida for the winter citrus harvest. Luis was an ageless child. He had a way of taking a deep weary drag on a cigarette, and after a long while letting the smoke curve slowly out of his nostrils. His face was wrinkled, marked with a tiny network of fragile lines at the corners of his eyes and deeper lines across his forehead.

Still a child, he liked to play games. He enjoyed the gaiety at the Christmas feast. But at the end of the working day, he would stand stooped over slightly with his hands stuck flat into his back pockets. From behind he looked like a dwarf, a tiny old man whose bones had dried up and warped with age.

Billy was the youngest of the children. He was not quite five but old enough to do a little work. He didn't earn much, but it was better, his father said, than having him sit around the day-care center costing them $.75 every single day. His mother kept the money he earned in a mason jar. When fall came, he'd get a pair of shoes if there was enough money. He could start school, if there was one nearby, in new shoes.

His brother lay beside him in the clearing. John was ten. In the years that separated Billy and John, a brother and sister had died, unnamed, a day after birth. John kept them alive in his imagination. There were few playmates in the camps and fields that he ever got to know.

"I got two brothers and a sister," he would say. "And they's all in heaven but Billy there.". . .

The man with the clipboard left. The children came out of the bushes, picked up their boxes. They bent over in silence and began to pluck at the vines. These are the children of harvest. "The kids that don't count" they are sometimes called. "The here-today-gone-tomorrow kids."

The Plight of the Children

Inspectors from the Department of Labor find children working illegally on 60 percent of the farms they inspect. And no one knows how many hide in the woods when it "looks like rain." No one really knows how many migrant children there are. Estimates run from 100,000 to 600,000. The most frequently used figure is 150,000. One survey in the olive groves of California showed that nearly three fourths of the workers were children. An Oregon survey showed the importance of the child's labor to the family. There the average migrant worker earned $32 a week during the weeks he worked. But his wife and children together earned $48. In some crops women and children do more than half the harvest work. . . .

Attempts at Assistance

There have been many brave attempts to provide migrant workers with medical service, usually on a shoestring budget and through the energy of a few determined people in a community. In the little farming towns around Morehead City, North Carolina, the Reverend Jack Mansfield got together the first mobile medical clinic, a white trailer called the Rocking Horse, equipped with the rudiments of a doctor's office. The Rocking Horse—so named because it tilted back and forth when you walked around in it—was staffed by a group of local doctors who took turns going out to the migrant camps. The welfare department was persuaded to provide a social worker. The National Council of Churches provided a migrant minister.

By the light of a flickering kerosene lantern, the lines of workers waited to see the doctor. Some had unnamed miseries of the head and the chest, aches and pains that move up the back and seize the neck in a vise. Colds, bad teeth, rheumatism, and chronic headaches could only be treated by the same white pills. . . .

Under the blue skies of Idaho, a twelve-year-old girl got her ponytail caught in a potato-digging machine. It ripped off her scalp, ears, eyelids, and cheeks. She died shortly afterward in a hospital. On a farm in California, a ten-year-old girl came back from the fields exhausted from a day's work. She fell asleep on a pile of burlap bags as she waited for her parents. As other workers returned from the fields, they tossed the empty bags on the stack, and the little girl was soon covered up. A two-ton truck backed across the pile and drove off. They did not find her body until the next day.

If children were mangled in steel mills, there would be a storm of public protest. But death and injury on the mechanized farms seem to pass unnoticed. Under the blue sky of the farm factory is no place for little children. Agriculture is one of the three most hazardous industries. In California alone, more than five hundred agricultural workers under the age of eighteen are seriously injured every year.

The migrants who follow the harvest are the only people in America who are desperate enough for this work to take it. Their children will be another generation of wanderers, lost to themselves and to the nation. . . .

The Invisible Army

Few urban Americans have any awareness of this vast impoverished army that tramps through their country to bring the crops in from the fields. It cannot be seen except as a broken-down car or bus here, a truck there, a ragged crew working somewhere off in a field.

But the harvest cycle yields its own fruits: ignorance, poverty, death, and despair. Until we see the connection between migrancy—the corpses piled up on the roadway, the children left to the darkness of ignorance and illiteracy, the despairing, destitute families groping for a way to live—and the bountiful supply of fruits and vegetables on every corner fruit stand or in every supermarket, no changes will come. Without this understanding, no war on poverty can hope to win more than a few skirmishes.

The Race to Put a Man in Space

By *Time*

In the aftermath of World War II, the United States was neither at war nor peace with what was then the Soviet Union. A sense of competition developed from this tense and unsteady relationship in which both nations worked to gain an advantage over the other in scientific and economic endeavors. In 1965 the United States was trying to catch up to the advanced Soviet space program. On June 3, *Gemini 4* launched astronauts Jim McDivitt and Ed White on a four-day space mission that included the first American space walk and helped to close the gap between the Soviet and U.S. space programs.

At the time, astronauts and space travel were relatively new and revolutionary ideas that captivated the imaginations of the American people. With the turmoil of war, protest and inequality that assailed the United States during the turbulent sixties, space travel allowed Americans the opportunity to turn their attention upward to the possibilities of the unknown. *Time* magazine reported frequently on the progress of the "space race" and included features on the personalities, backgrounds, and reactions of the first American astronauts to travel to the final frontier. These articles included detailed descriptions of the training and education required to become an astronaut, as well as information about space equipment, space communication, and even space food.

He stood on top of his spaceship's white titanium hull. He touched it with his bulky thermal gloves. He burned around like Buck Rogers propelling himself with his hand-held jet. He floated lazily on his back. He joked and laughed. He gazed down at the earth 103 miles below, spotted the Houston-Galveston Bay area where he lives and tried to take a picture of it. Like a gas station attendant, he checked the spacecraft's thrusters, wiped its windshield. Ordered to get back into the capsule, he protested like a scolded kid. "I'm doing great," he said. "It's fun. I'm not coming in." When, after 20 minutes of space gymnastics, U.S. Astronaut Edward Higgins White II, 34, finally did agree to squeeze himself back into his Gemini 4 ship, he still had not had enough of space walking. Said he to Command Pilot James Alton McDivitt: "It's the saddest day of my life."

White's exhilarating space stroll provided the moments of highest drama during Gemini 4's scheduled 62-orbit, 98-hour, 1,700,000-mile flight. White spent twice the time outside the spacecraft that Soviet Cosmonaut Aleksei Leonov did last March 18, and he had much more maneuverability; all Leonov did was somersault around at the end of a tether, getting dizzy, while White moved around pretty much at will.

Second Generation

Still, Gemini's planners would have scrubbed White's EVA (for Extra-Vehicular Activity) expedition in a second if they had thought it might detract from the flight's basic missions.

In Gemini 4, the U.S. took a big step toward closing the gap in the man-in-space race, in which the Soviet Union got off to a head start. More important, the flight signaled the advent of the second generation of U.S. spacecraft and spacemen. The two-man Gemini capsule is to the old Mercury capsule what a Thunderbird is to a Model T. Almost all previous U.S. space flights were pre-planned to the second, and any deviation meant trouble; in Gemini 4, the astronauts were given considerable flexibility, could and did change their plans and improvise at short notice. For the first time, a U.S. space flight was controlled from Houston's supersophisticated Manned Space Center, which makes Cape Kennedy almost as obsolete as a place once called Canaveral.

Moreover, the spacemen themselves were second generation. Project Mercury's pioneers were national legends almost before they got off the ground. Yet who, before last week, knew very much about Jim McDivitt and Ed White?

The Team

The pair made an almost perfect space team. Inside Man McDivitt is a superb pilot and a first-class engineer who is the son of an electrical engineer. Outside Man White is a daring flyer, a fine athlete, a military career–man who is the son of a retired Air Force major general who flew everything from balloons to jets.

McDivitt, whose 36th birthday is this week, is a whippet-lean (5 ft. 11 in., 155 lb.) Air Force major. . . .

As a jet fighter pilot, he went to Korea, flew 145 combat missions, won three Distinguished Flying Crosses and five Air Medals. In 1957 the Air Force sent him to the University of Michigan to get a degree in aeronautical engineering. . . . From Michigan he went to the Experimental Test Pilot School at Edwards Air Force Base in California, was selected for the X-15 testing program, but applied instead for Gemini.

He was picked with eight others—including Ed White—in September 1962. Jim McDivitt sounds about as dispassionate about being an astronaut as he would about fixing furnaces. "There's no magnet drawing me to the stars," he says flatly. "I look on this whole project as a real difficult technical problem—one that will require a lot of answers that must be acquired logically and in a step-by-step manner."

McDivitt may be able to keep his eyes off the stars, but not Ed White, also an Air Force major. White was an Army Air Forces brat, brought up at bases from the East Coast to Hawaii, and committed to flying for a livelihood. . . . White won an appointment to West Point, where he finished 128th in 1952's class of 523. He went to flight school in Florida and became a jet pilot.

White was—and is—a fanatic on physical fitness. . . . Of all the astronauts, he is considered by Gemini's medics to be the best physical specimen.

In 1957, while stationed in Germany, White read about the U.S.'s embryonic astronaut program, decided that he would one day get into it and, in the process of preparing himself, took a master's degree in aeronautical engineering at the University of Michigan—at the same time Jim McDivitt was there.

After Michigan, White went to test-pilot school, later was assigned to a necessary but frustratingly tangential job having to do with the space program. At the controls of a jet cargo plane, he would go into a screaming, precisely plotted dive that would create the zero-gravity weightlessness of a space ride. In this capacity, he helped in the training not only of John Glenn but of Ham and Enos, the chimpanzees who broke into space before men did. White figures that he "went weightless" 1,200 times—for a total of about five hours—before he was ever selected as a Gemini pilot.

In Gemini, White became smitten with a single overriding ambition: to be the first man on the moon. "His goal," says his father, "is to make that first flight."

Dress Rehearsals

Gemini officers picked McDivitt and White as the spacemen for last week's flight nearly a year ago. After that, each man spent scores of hours in a simulated capsule at Houston's Manned Spacecraft Center. They practiced the chilling procedures for aborting a flight in case of a mishap in a centrifuge at Johnsville, Pa. Together, they bobbed inside a Gemini capsule shell on the Gulf of Mexico off Galveston, rehearsing the act of opening the hatch, jumping out and inflating a life raft to await rescuers.

In preparation for his step-out into space, White spent 60 hours in vacuum chambers that simulated altitudes of up to 180,000 ft. Patiently, he practiced moving about in the suit he would wear outside the capsule. Weighing 31 lbs. and costing over $30,000, the garment is a marvel of cautious construction. With 22 layers, it acts as a coat of armor, as a heat repellant, as protection from deep-freeze temperatures, and as a pressure force to keep White's body from exploding in the near-vacuum of space. Yet it also allows a certain freedom of movement. Although NASA exports figured that the odds against White being punctured by a high-velocity micrometeor in space were about 10,000 to 1, they nevertheless blasted White's suit over and over again with splinters of plastic fired at 25,000 ft. per sec. In those tests, the suit held up.

No Mickey Mouse

White also spent some twelve hours rehearsing with his "hand-held self-maneuvering unit"—the gadget that was to help him walk around in space. The device weighs 7½ lbs., has two small cylinders of compressed oxygen belted to a handle that also acts as a trigger to send jets of air through two hollow tubes, each 2 ft.

long. Holding the contraption just below his midriff, White could, in his weightless state, manipulate it so as to send him, like a bit of fluff in the wind, in any direction he desired.

When, on May 25, only nine days before the launch date, NASA announced that White would try to take his walk in space, skeptics suggested that it was only a publicity gag. This irked the NASA men. "We're not playing Mickey Mouse with this thing," snapped Christopher Kraft, Gemini 4's mission director. "We're trying to carry out flight operations. I don't think it's very fair to suggest we're carrying out a propaganda stunt."

The Real Thing

Now the rehearsals were over, and it was time for the real thing. McDivitt and White were ready. "The condition of the astronauts is the best I've ever seen," said Dr. Charles Berry, Gemini's presiding physician. The countdown started 420 minutes before scheduled blast-off time, and as Mission Director Chris Kraft said, "Everything looks to be about as good as you could ever hope it to be."

Before dawn, McDivitt and White had a low-calorie breakfast of sirloin steak and eggs, gulped in breaths of pure oxygen to prevent the formation of nitrogen bubbles in their blood at high altitudes, went through the laborious process of putting on their space suits, and at 8:12 A.M. E.D.T. lay down on their twin bedlike couches in the capsule on Cape Kennedy's Launch Pad 19. The only hitch came 1 hr. 13 min. later, and 35 minutes before the scheduled launching time, when there was an electrical breakdown in the motor that was to lower the huge erector cradle, which had been used to set the Titan II booster rocket in its place. The delay lasted 1 hr. 16 min.

At 11:16 A.M. E.D.T., a billowing plume of hot orange smoke leaped from the base of the missile. Three seconds later, the rocket lifted ponderously from its pad, built speed rapidly as 430,000 lbs. of thrust propelled it skyward. As it rose, McDivitt and White lay in their seats, each clutching a D-shaped ring; by pulling on the rings, they could eject themselves instantly if they had to abort the mission.

As the first stage of the missile dropped away, the first words came from the capsule. Exclaimed McDivitt: "Beautiful!" Exclaimed White almost simultaneously: "Beautiful!" Every word, every breath and every heartbeat of McDivitt and White as well as every calibration on every instrument in the cabin were under constant surveillance in Houston's new $170 million Manned Spacecraft Center.

There the nerve center for the Gemini flight was a softly lighted, air-conditioned Mission Operations Control building, where some 300 scientists, engineers, doctors and technicians hunched over blinking panels or watched the orbital progress on 10-ft. by 60-ft. screens. Chris Kraft and his men were linked through 10,000 miles of wire, 140 instrument consoles and 384 television receivers with the entire Gemini 4 communications operation—including 11,000 men in a recovery fleet of ships and planes spanning two oceans. Basic to control of the Gemini 4 flight were five IBM 7094-II computers, each of which could digest 50,000 "bits" of telemetry information per second from the orbiting craft. Gemini is able to flash back 275 different kinds of information, three times more than Mercury; the computer gobbles it up, puts it on paper or, upon specific demand, transmits it by television to the mission control officials.

Watching It Go

Gemini 4's ascent went precisely according to plan: accelerating to 17,500 m.p.h., the spacecraft entered into an orbit that took it 175 miles high at apogee, 100 miles high at perigee. At 6 min. 6 sec. from lift-off, Command Pilot McDivitt set off a string of explosive bolts that set the capsule free from its second-stage booster. The booster dropped loose and McDivitt Swung Gemini 4 around so that it was flying blunt end forward. The booster, tumbling slightly and moving slower than the capsule, dropped about 400 ft. below. . . .

McDivitt manipulated the capsule's Orbit Attitude Maneuvering System (OAMS) comprised of 16 rocket engines mounted about the capsule to allow changes in altitude and direction. The fuel supply for OAMS was separate from the crucial fuel cache McDivitt would need to fire the retrorockets for his return to earth later on.

The craft headed over Mexico toward the end of its first orbit. The ship's OAMS fuel supply had gone from 410 lbs. to 288 lbs. in the hide-and-seek game with the booster. Director Kraft told McDivitt to take it easy on the fuel in chasing the errant booster. The astronaut replied: "It's out farther than we expected." A little later he asked Houston, "Do you want a major effort to close with this thing or save the fuel?" The instant answer: save the fuel and forget about the booster. Resigned, McDivitt said, "I guess we're just going to have to watch it go away."

By now, Gemini 4 was over the coast of Africa, well into its second orbit—the orbit in which Ed White was supposed to get out and walk around.

White began to ready his EVA gear. There were 54 items to check from his flight-plan list, and it was painfully slow going. White began to perspire heavily; almost every drop of sweat was noted by Houston's wizard gear. As the craft flew over Australia McDivitt radioed the tracking station there: "We don't have any time at all." From Houston, Kraft told him to delay White's EVA mission until the third revolution.

And out He Went

As Gemini 4 went into its third orbit, White donned his EVA equipment. He snapped on an extra face plate which was tinted gold to deflect the sun's broiling rays, hooked up his gold-coated umbilical cord—a 24.3-ft. tether connecting him to the spaceship, providing him with oxygen and a space-walk talk system. Since he could not look down with his helmet on, White used a mirror to strap on to his chest a shoebox-sized pack weighing 8.3 lbs. and containing a twelve-minute supply of emergency oxygen. If his main oxygen source failed, Spaceman White could flip a switch on the box, haul himself back into the spacecraft, close the hatch and hurriedly repressurize the cabin before his portable supply ran out. . . .

Now Gemini 4 was 4 hr. 43 min. off the launching pad. It was flying blunt end forward and upside down in relation to the earth—although this made no difference to the astronauts in their weightless condition.

Slowly, White began cranking a ratchet handle to loosen a set of prongs around the hatch opening. The hatch was free. It raised to a 50° angle, and White poked his head through the opening. McDivitt asked Director Kraft for a go-ahead. Replied Kraft: "Tell him we're ready for him to go whenever he is." Out went White.

Gripping his jet gun, he slipped alone into space over the Pacific, just east of Hawaii. On the part of his space suit facing the sun, the temperature was an infernal 250° above zero; on the shady side, 150° below zero. White punched the trigger on his hand jet, squirted himself under the capsule, then back to the top. His movements jostled the ship. McDivitt, carefully working the controls inside Gemini 4 to maintain a stable base for White, said into his microphone to Gemini 3 Astronaut Virgil ("Gus") Grissom at Houston control center: "One thing about it, when Ed gets out there and starts whipping around, it sure makes the spacecraft tough to control."

Along the Life Line

By the time he had been out of the capsule for three minutes, White had exhausted his hand gun's fuel propellant. This was neither alarming nor surprising, since NASA officials had purposely kept the thrust of the gadget low and the fuel supply at a minimum for this first experimental trip. From then on, White maneuvered by twisting his torso and hand-pulling himself back and forth along his life line.

As Gemini 4 streaked toward the West Coast of the U.S., White reported: "I'm looking right down, and it looks like we're coming on the coast of California. There is absolutely no disorientation association."

White had a 35-mm. camera attached to his hand jet, and McDivitt had a 16-mm. movie camera attached to the spacecraft interior and fixed to peer out through the window. Grissom reminded them from the ground: "Take some pictures." McDivitt said to White: "Get out in front where I can see you again." White moved to a better position and Grissom told the space walker: "You've got about five minutes." But Ed White was enjoying himself immensely: "The sun in space is not blinding but it's quite nice. I'm coming back down on the spacecraft. I can sit out here and see the whole California coast."

"Right over Houston"

A few moments later, McDivitt cried excitedly to Grissom: "Hey, Gus, I don't know if you read us, but we're right over Houston." White chimed in: "We're looking right down on Houston." McDivitt to White: "Go on out and look. Yeah, that's Galveston Bay right there. Hey, Ed, can you see it on your side of the spacecraft?" White: "I'll get a picture."

Discussing their photographic endeavors, White told McDivitt: "I've only shot about three or four." Said McDivitt: "All right, I've taken a lot, but they're not very good. You're in too close for most of them. I finally put the focus down to about eight feet or so."

The two kept chattering over VOX, a voice-activated system that cut off messages from controllers on earth whenever McDivitt and White were conversing. Again and again Grissom tried to break through: "Gemini 4, Houston. Gemini 4, Houston." The space twins kept talking to each other. Finally, McDivitt acknowledged the calls from earth: "Got any messages for us?"

Grissom burst in urgently: "Gemini 4, get back in!" McDivitt replied: "O.K. We're trying to come back in now." Grissom, more calmly now: "Roger, we've been trying to talk to you for a while here."

McDivitt: "Back in. Come on."

White: "Hate to come back to you, but I'm coming.". . .

Tired, Safe, and Elated

Grissom chimed in again: "Gemini 4, Houston." White: "I'm fixing to come in the house." McDivitt: "Any message for us, Houston?" Grissom: "Yeah! Get back in!" McDivitt: "He's standing in the seat now and his legs are down below the instrument panel." Grissom: "O.K. Get him back in now." McDivitt: "He's coming in. He's having some trouble getting back in the space cabin, looks like." Grissom: "You got your cabin lights up bright in case you hit darkness?"

Moments later, White was back inside—tired but safe and elated as Gemini 4 sped through the black night over the eastern Atlantic Ocean.

The Medical Report

NASA officials in Houston were delighted at the EVA performance. Medically, White had responded well. His usual on-the-ground pulse beat of 50 soared to 178 as he re-entered the capsule, but that was not considered dangerous under the circumstances. When reporters asked if White might have become euphoric during his voyage, Dr. Berry quickly said: "I think it's just elation at being out there, doing this task."

As the flight went into the weekend, the medical texts continued. Dr. Berry was particularly concerned about orthostatic hypertension, a drop in blood pressure combined with an abnormally rapid heartbeat, which can bring on fainting spells. "What this means," said Berry, "is that the cardiovascular system simply gets lazy because the heart doesn't have to work anywhere nearly as hard to circulate the blood. In weightlessness, there's no pressure on the heart—being a muscle, it gets lazy and merely does what it needs to do."

Throughout their flight, both White and McDivitt did nip-ups. Using a "bungee cord"—a tough length of rubber with a loop at one end, a T handle at the other—the astronauts put their feet in the loop, pulled up on the handle 30 times in 30 seconds. It took 60 lbs. of force to stretch the rubber. For comparison purposes, White was to exercise four times a day, McDivitt just once. Before the flight was half over, McDivitt requested—and received— permission to exercise more often. "I just haven't moved around very much," he said.

Dehydration was another potential danger, and the Houston controllers often reminded White and McDivitt that they should take a drink of water. Astronauts require at least two quarts of water a day—more than double the usual earth-bound need—because their space suits' cooling systems evaporate perspiration as it forms, thus increasing the loss of body fluids. If McDivitt and White failed to drink their quota, they could return to earth as wrinkled as prunes.

The menu aloft included dishes such as beef pot roast, banana pudding and fruitcake. It even catered to McDivitt's Roman Catholicism by having fish dishes for Friday. But the food was less than tasty: either freeze-dried or dehydrated, it was mixed with water in plastic bags, kneaded until it became mushy, and it had all the consistency of baby food.

Sanitation was another problem. Neither astronaut could shave during the flight. They had only small, damp wash rags with which to mop their faces. Liquid body wastes went overboard through a urine transfer system. Solid wastes were stored in the craft in self-sealing bags containing disinfectant pills.

Party Line

Once the excitement of White's walk beyond the capsule had subsided, both astronauts took four-hour naps. Because they could not turn the volume in their headsets all the way down, they were occasionally jarred from sleep by radio transmissions from the ground. . . .

Both the astronauts' wives got on the line for four minutes.

When McDivitt's wife Pat came on the radio, he said, "I'm

over California right now." She said, "Get yourself over Texas." He asked her: "Behaving yourself?" She said, "I'm always good. Are you being good?" McDivitt replied, "I don't have much space. About all I can do is look out the window." When White's wife, also named Pat, got the mike, she said, "It looked like you were having a wonderful time yesterday." White said, "Quite a time. Quite a time." Mrs. White said, "I can't wait to talk to you about it." White replied, "O.K., honey, I'll see you later.". . .

On their 22nd revolution, White and McDivitt broke the American record in space—34 hr. 20 min.—set by Gordon Cooper's Faith 7 flight on May 15, 1963. "I would like to congratulate you on the new American space-flight record," said the controller in Houston. Laconically, White said, "We got a few more to go."

Ready for More

As the flight sped into its third day, the orbit held fairly firm with a 173-mile apogee and a 101-mile perigee, indicating that Gemini 4 could stay aloft well into this week.

Life aboard Gemini 4 settled into a routine that seemed almost mundane after Ed White's excursion into raw space. Yet even as the mission continued to circle the earth, there was new Project Gemini activity. Work had begun at Cape Kennedy to mount and prepare another Titan II missile, topped by another spacecraft: Gemini 5, which will carry Astronauts Gordon Cooper and Charles Conrad on a seven-day space expedition in late August.

After the Project Gemini series will come Project Apollo, aimed at landing an American man on the moon in its first shot some time in 1970. But the man on the moon is only the beginning of the Apollo program. After that, it will send the spaceship many millions of miles on the way to the planets.

The Challenge of Equality

By Lyndon B. Johnson

On June 4, 1965, President Lyndon B. Johnson delivered the commencement address at Howard University in Washington, D.C. President Johnson spoke to the predominantly black graduates about the great challenge of establishing racial equality within the United States. In his speech, he warned his audience that while the "scars" of slavery and prejudice were damaging to Americans of all races, the black graduates would have to "rely mostly on [their] own efforts" to overcome the damaging effects of racism.

Using statistics to illustrate the difference between white and black Americans in matters of education, income, infant mortality, and poverty, Johnson challenged the Howard graduating class of 1965 to work diligently in order to eradicate the prevalent social and economic inequality. President Johnson spoke about recent legislation, such as the Voter's Rights Act, that established better opportunities for underprivileged minorities. Delivered at the midway point of that tumultuous year, President Johnson's speech was ominously prophetic in its warning that unresolved inequality would lead to riot and unrest. However, he also promised that the success of the hardworking graduates of Howard University would light a "candle of understanding" that would never go out.

Lyndon B. Johnson, Howard University commencement address, Washington, D.C., June 4, 1965.

Our earth is the home of revolution.

In every corner of every continent men charged with hope contend with ancient ways in pursuit of justice. They reach for the newest of weapons to realize the oldest of dreams: that each may walk in freedom and pride, stretching his talents, enjoying the fruits of the earth.

Our enemies may occasionally seize the day of change. But it is the banner of our revolution they take. And our own future is linked to this process of swift and turbulent change in many lands. But nothing, in any country, touches us more profoundly, nothing is more freighted with meaning for our own destiny, than the revolution of the Negro American.

In far too many ways American Negroes have been another nation: deprived of freedom, crippled by hatred, the doors of opportunity closed to hope.

In our time change has come to this nation too. Heroically, the American Negro—acting with impressive restraint—has peacefully protested and marched, entered the courtrooms and the seats of government, demanding a justice long denied. The voice of the Negro was the call to action. But it is a tribute to America that, once aroused, the courts and the Congress, the President and most of the people, have been the allies of progress.

Thus we have seen the high court of the country declare that discrimination based on race was repugnant to the Constitution, and therefore void. We have seen—in 1957, 1960, and again in 1964—the first civil rights legislation in almost a century.

As majority leader I helped guide two of these bills through the Senate. And, as your President, I was proud to sign the third.

And soon we will have the fourth new law, guaranteeing every American the right to vote.

No act of my administration will give me greater satisfaction than the day when my signature makes this bill too the law of the land.

The voting rights bill will be the latest, and among the most important, in a long series of victories. But this victory—as Winston Churchill said of another triumph for freedom—"is not the end. . . . It is not even the beginning of the end. But it is, perhaps, the end of the beginning."

That beginning is freedom; and the barriers to that freedom are tumbling. Freedom is the right to share, fully and equally, in American society—to vote, to hold a job, to enter a public place, to go to school. It is the right to be treated, in every part of our national life, as a man equal in dignity and promise to all others.

Opportunity Is Essential, but Not Enough

But freedom is not enough. You do not wipe away the scars of centuries by saying: Now, you are free to go where you want, do as you desire, and choose the leaders you please.

You do not take a man who, for years, has been hobbled by chains, liberate him, bring him to the starting line of a race, saying "you are free to compete with all the others," and still justly believe you have been completely fair.

Thus it is not enough to open the gates of opportunity. All our citizens must have the ability to walk through those gates.

This is the next and the more profound stage of the battle for civil rights. We seek not just freedom but opportunity—not just legal equity but human ability—not just equality as a right and a theory, but equality as a fact and a result.

For the task is to give twenty million Negroes the same chance as every other American to learn and grow, to work and share in society, to develop their abilities—physical, mental and spiritual—and to pursue their individual happiness.

To this end equal opportunity is essential, but not enough. Men and women of all races are born with the same range of abilities. But ability is not just the product of birth. It is stretched or stunted by the family you live with, and the neighborhood you live in—by the school you go to, and the poverty or richness of your surroundings. It is the product of a hundred unseen forces playing upon the infant, the child, and the man.

This graduating class at Howard University is witness to the indomitable determination of the Negro American to win his way in American life.

The number of Negroes in schools of high learning has almost doubled in fifteen years. The number of nonwhite professional workers has more than doubled in ten years. The median income of Negro college women now exceeds that of white college women. And these are the enormous accomplishments of distinguished individual Negroes—many of them graduates of this institution.

These are proud and impressive achievements. But they only tell the story of a growing middle class minority, steadily narrowing the gap between them and their white counterparts.

But for the great majority of Negro Americans—the poor, the unemployed, the uprooted and dispossessed—there is a grimmer story. They still are another nation. Despite the court orders and the laws, the victories and speeches, for them the walls are rising and the gulf is widening.

Here are some of the facts of this American failure.

Thirty-five years ago the rate of unemployment for Negroes and whites was about the same. Today the Negro rate is twice as high.

In 1948 the 8 percent unemployment rate for Negro teenage boy was actually less than that of whites. By last year it had grown to 23 percent, as against 13 percent for whites.

Between 1949 and 1959, the income of Negro men relative to white men declined in every section of the country. From 1952 to 1963 the median income of Negro families compared to white actually dropped from 57 percent to 53 percent.

In the years 1955–57, 22 percent of experienced Negro workers were out of work at some time during the year. In 1961–63 that proportion had soared to 29 percent.

Since 1947 the number of white families living in poverty has decreased 27 percent while the number of poor nonwhite families went down only 3 percent.

The infant mortality of nonwhites in 1940 was 70 percent greater than whites. Twenty-two years later it was 90 percent greater.

Moreover, the isolation of Negro from white communities is increasing, rather than diminishing as Negroes crowd into the central cities—becoming a city within a city.

The Reasons We Are Losing Ground

Of course Negro Americans as well as white Americans have shared in our rising national abundance. But the harsh fact of the matter is that in the battle for true equality too many are losing ground.

We are not completely sure why this is. The causes are complex and subtle. But we do know the two broad basic reasons. And we know we have to act.

First, Negroes are trapped—as many whites are trapped—in inherited, gateless poverty. They lack training and skills. They are shut in slums, without decent medical care. Private and public poverty combine to cripple their capacities.

We are attacking these evils through our poverty program, our education program, our health program and a dozen more—aimed at the root causes of poverty.

We will increase, and accelerate, and broaden this attack in years to come, until this most enduring of foes yields to our unyielding will.

But there is a second cause—more difficult to explain, more deeply grounded, more desperate in its force. It is the devastating heritage of long years of slavery; and a century of oppression, hatred and injustice.

For Negro poverty is not white poverty. Many of its causes and many of its cures are the same. But there are differences—deep, corrosive, obstinate differences—radiating painful roots into the community, the family, and the nature of the individual.

These differences are not racial differences. They are solely and simply the consequence of ancient brutality, past injustice, and present prejudice. They are anguishing to observe. For the Negro they are a reminder of oppression. For the white they are a reminder of guilt. But they must be faced, and dealt with, and overcome; if we are to reach the time when the only difference between Negroes and whites is the color of their skin.

Nor can we find a complete answer in the experience of other American minorities. They made a valiant, and largely successful effort to emerge from poverty and prejudice. The Negro, like these others, will have to rely mostly on his own efforts. But he cannot do it alone. For they did not have the heritage of centuries to overcome. They did not have a cultural tradition which had been twisted and battered by endless years of hatred and hopelessness. Nor were they excluded because of race or color—a feeling whose dark intensity is matched by no other prejudice in our society.

Nor can these differences be understood as isolated infirmities. They are a seamless web. They cause each other. They result from each other. They reinforce each other. Much of the Negro community is buried under a blanket of history and circumstance. It is not a lasting solution to lift just one corner. We must stand on all sides and raise the entire cover if we are to liberate our fellow citizens.

One of the differences is the increased concentration of Negroes in our cities. More than 73 percent of all Negroes live in urban areas compared with less than 70 percent of whites. Most of them live in slums. And most of them live together; a separated people. Men are shaped by their world. When it is a world of decay ringed by an invisible wall—when escape is arduous and uncertain, and the saving pressures of a more hopeful society are unknown—it can cripple the youth and desolate the man.

There is also the burden a dark skin can add to the search for a productive place in society. Unemployment strikes most swiftly and broadly at the Negro. This burden erodes hope. Blighted hope breeds despair. Despair brings indifference to the learning which offers a way out. And despair coupled with indifference is often the source of destructive rebellion against the fabric of society.

There is also the lacerating hurt of early collision with white hatred or prejudice, distaste or condescension. Other groups have felt similar intolerance. But success and achievement could wipe it away. They do not change the color of a man's skin. I have seen this uncomprehending pain in the eyes of young Mexican-American school children. It can be overcome. But, for many, the wounds are always open.

Family Breakdown

Perhaps most important—its influence radiating to every part of life—is the breakdown of the Negro family structure. For this, most of all, white America must accept responsibility. It flows from centuries of oppression and persecution of the Negro man. It flows from the long years of degradation and discrimination which have attacked his dignity and assaulted his ability to provide for his family.

This, too, is not pleasant to look upon. But it must be faced by those whose serious intent is to improve the life of all Americans.

Only a minority—less than half—of all Negro children reach the age of 18 having lived all their lives with both parents. At this moment, today, little less than two-thirds are living with both parents. Probably a majority of all Negro children receive federally-aided public assistance during their childhood.

The family is the cornerstone of our society. More than any other force it shapes the attitude, the hopes, the ambitions, and the values of the child. When the family collapses the child is usually damaged. When it happens on a massive scale the community itself is crippled.

Unless we work to strengthen the family—to create conditions under which most parents will stay together—all the rest: schools and playgrounds, public assistance and private concern—will not be enough to cut completely the circle of despair and deprivation.

There is no single easy answer to all these problems.

Jobs are part of the answer. They bring the income which permits a man to provide for his family.

Decent homes in decent surroundings and a chance to learn are part of the answer.

Welfare and social programs better designed to hold families together are part of the answer.

Care for the sick is part of the answer.

An understanding heart by all Americans is also part of the answer.

To all these fronts—and a dozen more—I will dedicate the expanding efforts of my administration.

A Proposed Conference

But there are other answers still to be found. Nor do we fully understand all the problems. Therefore, this fall, I intend to call a White House Conference of scholars, experts, Negro leaders, and officials at every level of government.

Its theme and title: *"To Fulfill These Rights."*

Its object: to help the American Negro fulfill the rights which—after the long time of injustice—he is finally about to secure.

- to move beyond opportunity to achievement.
- to shatter forever, not only the barriers of law and public practice, but the walls which bound the condition of man by the color of his skin.
- to dissolve, as best we can, the antique enmities of the heart which diminish the holder, divide the great democracy, and do wrong to the children of God.

I pledge this will be a chief goal of my Administration, and of my program next year, and in years to come.

I hope it will be part of the program of all America.

For what is justice?

It is to fulfill the fair expectations of man.

Thus, American justice is a very special thing. For, from the first, this has been a land of towering expectations. It was to be a nation where each man would be ruled by the common consent of all—enshrined in law, given life by institutions, guided by men themselves subject to its rule. And all—of every station and origin—would be touched equally in obligation and in liberty.

Beyond the law lay the land. It was a rich land, glowing with more abundant promise than ever man had seen. Here, unlike any place yet known, all were to share the harvest.

And beyond this was the dignity of man. Each could become whatever his qualities of mind and spirit would permit—to strive, to seek, and, if he could, to find his happiness.

This is American justice. We have pursued it faithfully to the edge of our imperfections. And we have failed to find it for the American Negro.

It is the glorious opportunity of this generation to end the one huge wrong of the American nation—and in so doing to find America for ourselves, with the same immense thrill of discovery which gripped those who first began to realize that here, at last, was a home for freedom.

All it will take is for all of us to understand what this country is and what it must become.

The Scripture promises: "I shall light a candle of understanding in thine heart, which shall not be put out."

Together, and with millions more, we can light that candle of understanding in the heart of America.

And, once lit, it will never again go out.

The White House Festival of the Arts Backfires

By Saul Maloff

Amidst the turmoil of protest and war in 1965, most Americans went about life as usual. Even the White House tried to continue with domestic affairs, carrying on a dizzying schedule of festivities and meetings like any other administration. As part of President Johnson's "Great Society," he pledged greater federal support to the arts. The Johnson administration extended this support by inviting artists, writers, and musicians to attend the First White House Festival of the Arts, an event designed to honor American artists with an evening of dinner and entertainment at the White House. However, when the U.S. poet laureate, Robert Lowell, withdrew his initial acceptance and sent an open letter to President Johnson explaining that because of the government's involvement in Vietnam and its foreign policy in general, he would not attend the festival, other artists either followed his example or chose to attend in order to denounce the government's policy. Saul Maloff attended the White House Festival of the Arts on June 14 and witnessed how Lowell's open letter turned the first festival into a forum for protest.

Saul Maloff, "Art and Vietnam: The White House Festival," *Commonweal*, vol. LXXXII, July 9, 1965, pp. 485–87. Copyright © 1965 by Commonweal Publishing Co., Inc. Reproduced by permission.

If institutions, like some warm-blooded animals, can learn from experience, the First White House Festival of the Arts, which unfolded in mournful numbers on June 14, is likely to be the last. In nearly all respects, the event (or concoction, or pseudo-event) was a catastrophe from which the nation's image—the cant term seems proper—will be a long time recovering. As a display of our cultural wares, or booty, it was simply vulgar when it was not funny—which is not to say there was nothing good in the bursting supermarket assembled for the splashy spectacular; and as a political occasion, it was a grievous and ghastly embarrassment.

Lowell's Letter

And let no man say the day was not political. Whether or not its conception was triggered by the disaffection of the intellectuals and its dramatization by the recent Washington teach-in—meant as a kind of conciliatory gesture, as some people speculated—is not the point. All events which take place in the White House, even international convocations of landscape gardeners, are political. But leaving aside all ponderous theoretical questions of the relations of art and power, culture and politics, an event which appeared otherwise destined for the oblivion of the society pages was transfigured suddenly and shockingly and given solemn meaning when, a week or so earlier, Robert Lowell, our first poet, reconsidered his impetuous initial acceptance of the invitation to participate and informed the President in his now-famous open letter that he could not in conscience attend, that merely by being there his presence might seem to signify some "subtle" endorsement of a foreign policy which he deplored. To an extraordinary degree, Lowell's grave and potent act colored all the proceedings, both high-serious and low-comic, background and foreground.

The accelerating events in the background threatened to reduce the event itself to anti-climax. Immediately following publication of the Lowell letter, a group of the best novelists and poets and artists in the country, none of whom had been asked to the White House, issued a statement in support of Lowell. Of the other invited writers, John Hersey and Saul Bellow, while stating, each in his way, their misgivings concerning Vietnam and Santo Domingo, announced they would accept. Later that week, Arthur Schlesinger Jr., in an address to a booksellers' convention in Washington, went out of his way to lecture Lowell on manners and moral responsibilty. Philip Roth, in a letter to the *Times*, suggested that there was something incongruous about an arts-festival sponsored by an administration "so insensitive to human values" (in its foreign policy); and, concluding his rebuke to Schlesinger, left to each man "his own sense of the ridiculous." The full story of the wrath of writers during that charged week must await telling another time.

Tension at the Festival

On Sunday, June 13, at a White House "rehearsal" for the gala event, Mark Van Doren, who was to chair the readings, read a statement in which he explicitly identified himself with Lowell's position. Then, for unexplained reasons which one may specu-late upon, as many did, Mr. Van Doren chose the next day to cur-tail the length and modify the tone of his statement, saying only that Lowell must be respected for acting as his conscience dic-tated, and leaving all the rest at the level of implication.

Hersey, however, was not content with implication. Before reading two of the more chilling passages from his *Hiroshima*, he spoke meaningly and in measured tones of a reliance on mil-itary power, of national arrogance, of fateful miscalculations which could lead step by inexorable step to what he was about to describe. Bellow made no statement. He read a carefully se-lected letter from *Herzog* and let it go at that. Phyllis McGinley added a new verse to an old poem in which she asked that we all be tolerant of poets even when they are "troublesome." The word rhymed with "bubblesome." In the absence of Lowell, Miss McGinley, who made the cover of *Time* that very day, repre-sented American poetry on that day-long tribute to the national genius. So tense was the atmosphere in the White House theater, where the readings took place, that when Catherine Drinker Bowen read some pleasant little anecdotes from her pleasantly anecdotal little book on Mr. Justice Holmes, the audience laughed excessively and with vast relief.

The tone of the day had been fatally set. After a brief respite, the guests in their hundreds were whisked away in military buses to the National Gallery of Art for an excellent lunch and an un-fortunate address by George Kennan, who came all the way from Vienna to tell his listeners that some artists were oddballs with eccentric ways, and that the artist had a duty—if he expected so-ciety to pay heed; and, indeed, to *pay*—to "communicate" and all that. It all had a terribly familiar ring. Artists know only too well that the reasonable-sounding word has contained, historically, a veiled threat; and in the command to "communicate" there lurks the death of all that is adventurous in the artistic enterprise. Moreover, Mr. Kennan, after putting Goethe to odd uses, called upon artists to "shield the public from artistic frivolity and charlatanism" and "protect art from debasement at the hands of the indecencies: not just the indecencies in the sense of pornography (though these, too), but indecencies of exhibitionism, of sensation-hunting, of cheap trickery of all sorts." If artists already had grave doubts about the role of government in the arts, they will find scant reason for comfort in Kennan's remarks.

Familiar Tunes

Full—if not rich—is the word for the afternoon's cultural bazaar. Timed to the minute, the arts were unfurled in all their gorgeous panoply. Here one minute, gone the next; and nothing new, nothing surprising, nothing fresh—entertainment, really, for the weary postprandial travellers. The Louisville Orchestra played some rather lively pieces by Ned Rorem, and a concertina by its conductor, Robert Whitney, that was correct, polite, soporific. The lovely Roberta Peters sang a song by Bernstein, another by Gershwin (as a matter of fact, "Summertime"); and some brief scenes were enacted from two current Broadway productions—"The Subject Was Roses" and "The Glass Menagerie." Mildred Dunnock played some affecting moments from "Death of a Salesman"; and some snippets were shown, each prefaced by some tiresome remarks narrated by Charlton Heston, though he was not responsible for the script, from Hitchcock's "North by Northwest," Kazan's "On the Waterfront," Stevens' "Shane," Wyler's "Friendly Persuasion," and Zinnemann's "High Noon." The effect on the whole was rather like listening to familiar tunes from old favorites—the whistleable parts. By far the most powerful moment of the afternoon was provided by Moses Gunn, the fine young Negro actor, in a brutal and funny scene from Millard Lampell's "Hard Travelin'" which had some hard things to say about being black and staying alive and human.

End of a Full Day

The exhibition of painting and sculpture was, for the most part, splendid, if expected—revealing the entrenched modes of abstraction at their best. But so inadequately were the paintings hung in their narrow, cramping corridor, and so incongruously were some of the sculptures situated in the tame, trimmed gardens and lawns, as to neutralize, and diminish, much of their force. Similarly, the photographs were in nearly all instances the predictable classics of the form; and, again, they overpowered their allotted space.

It may be making too much of a ferocity of stride and sternness of manner to say that President Johnson seemed not altogether happy to be there even for a few moments. (The gracious, gallant, enduring First Lady was continuously present.) Yet, whatever his feelings, the President, in his brief talk, uttered the profoundest truth of the long, hard day. Enumerating what the government might "do" for the arts and its practitioners, he began by saying that, in the first place, it should leave artists alone. In the circumstances, that seemed an excellent idea.

Robert Joffrey's dancers were young, charming, agile, even if they were not enterprising. At that point, nothing could have stirred the noisy, restless, unheeding audience. Everyone was looking toward the refreshments bar, and the nearest exit. Finally, the great Duke Ellington came on to try to beat some life into the dead horse; but it was too late. And too little. He put down a sound that had been superseded by at least eight turnings in the history of American jazz—a big, brassy sound that must have seemed archaic even to that audience. It was as far removed from the "new thing" as Frank Gilroy is from Genet and Beckett.

The rich, full day ended on a curious rustic note. Out on the far lawn, close by the refreshments, Dwight MacDonald gave a stunning demonstration of human resiliency. Having begun by lending his name to the statement in support of Lowell, he had gone on to say, in a letter to *Time* magazine, that he felt he could best serve his President and his country by accepting the White House's belated invitation—though he did not and would not, of course, disavow Lowell, and even though Lowell had said in his letter that in declining the invitation he felt he was best serving both President and country.

Accept MacDonald did. And having drunk his host's wine and eaten his host's food, he forthwith circulated a statement right there and then knocking his host's foreign policy. One suspects that the President may have felt ill-served, and the country astonished at that bizarre spectacle of moral legerdemain. But it was getting on to midnight then; and, as the last, lingering guests slowly and unsteadily departed, the chill, sweet, surprised night settled on the trouble scene, concealing for the time being only some of the shallower wounds. The night knew that you can't trust writers and artists. They are ungrateful; some, at their best, are dangerous; and some may even bite the hand that feeds them.

Only Robert Lowell spoke his heart and stayed home—and by his superb symbolic act reminded us of the few remaining possibilities of high style and austere dignity, and of the urgencies of the spirit.

The Other Side of Feminism

By Marion K. Sanders

The 1960s was a decade in which people began to speak out. From year to year, a growing number of social groups began to voice their demand for equal rights and equal opportunity. Every voice that asked for justice heard at least one resounding reply of opposition—sometimes from groups of differing viewpoints, sometimes from people who once seemed to be on the same side of the issue. The backlash was felt by the growing number of feminists who spoke out against the unequal treatment of women in American society. In 1963 Betty Friedan published a controversial feminist manifesto entitled *The Feminine Mystique.* In 1965 many women began to vocalize their dissatisfaction with the book, despite its popular success. One such woman was Marion K. Sanders, a writer for *Harper's Magazine* who openly disagreed with Friedan's assertion that women would be happier, healthier members of society if they joined the workforce rather than stay at home. During the first half of 1965, Sanders researched the subject by interviewing women who had successful careers and women who remained in the home. The women interviewed also included a cross section of different races and social backgrounds. While referring often to the themes of *The Feminine Mystique*, Sanders presents a very negative view of the feminist allure.

Marion K. Sanders, "The New American Female: Demi-Feminism Takes Over," *Harper's Magazine*, vol. 231, July 19, 1965, pp. 37–43. Copyright © 1965 by Harper's Magazine. All rights reserved. Reproduced by permission.

L ike the Vice President, the First Lady tailors her job to suit herself—and the President. She is not, however, a free agent, for the Chief Executive's wife is the sole source of copy for the industrious lady reporters who cover the White House. Even if she loafs on the job, they work hard to make her a symbol of contemporary female-ness. Often they succeed. Thus Mamie Eisenhower, in her pink inaugural gown and little-girl bangs, was a kind of corn-fed Queen Victoria beaming upon the bland domesticity that engulfed the nation's postwar brides. Jacqueline Kennedy—an eighteenth-century type like all the Kennedy ladies—was a latter-day Great Whig Hostess. She satisfied an affluent generation's craving for gorgeous entertainments, court hairdressers, riding to hounds, and salons filled with fashionable wits and dandies.

"John Kennedy just didn't understand career women," a warm admirer of the late President said recently. This was natural enough since he scarcely knew any.

Lyndon B. Johnson, on the other hand, is married to one. Miz Johnson—as he and her staff are apt to call her—has, among other things, managed a TV station and parlayed a modest inheritance into a hefty fortune. "Women doers" are high style in Washington and the President has declared war on "male curmudgeonism" in the federal service.

To be sure, Ladybird has turned in her uniform in the pro league. "She works for nothing," the President confessed to a gathering of female eminences. Her amateur standing does not seem to oppress the First Lady. Some weeks ago I trailed her on a dawn-to-dusk safari that started at 6:00 A.M. in the company of a planeload of news-hungry reporters. En route, she chatted individually with each of them. As the day wore on, she made three speeches, presented diplomas to domestic Peace Corps trainees, visited a remedial reading class and toured a rural slum, pausing on the way to accommodate the whims of a rabble of TV cameramen, indigenous small fry, deserving Democrats, and surprised matrons in mink who had never seen anything quite like this before. It was a virtuoso performance, sustained for seventeen hours. When it was over, she flew off to the ranch for "a walk under the sky"—as she put it—and a domestic weekend with a husband whose idea of relaxation is a two-hundred-guest barbecue.

I don't know what the Johnsons talk about in their private moments, if any. But I can vouch that at the White House breakfast table or on the banks of the Pedernales there are no debates about whether or not it is "feminine" for a woman to make political speeches, drive a tractor, or head a government agency.

Perhaps these issues never came up in Texas, which in bygone years was known as fine country for men and dogs but hell on women and horses. Frontiersmen respected the wives and steeds who survived these rigors. It was from Texas in 1875 that Mrs. Sarah W. Hiatt reported to the National Women's party: "There is a great liberality here of sentiment concerning the avocations of women. Though the right of women to the ballot seems to be a new idea to our people, I have never lived in a community where the women are more nearly abreast of men in all the activities of life. . . ."

This "liberality of sentiment" is in the air of Washington today. It is felt particularly by the women who have long toiled in drab obscurity in the old-line government agencies. They have new hairdos and a new gleam in their eyes. The President has given some two thousand of them a long-overdue boost up the civil-service ladder, and is still looking the field over. It is a heady atmosphere according to Ruth Van Cleve, recently appointed director of the Interior Department's Office of Territories. "For years I was just a government lawyer in sensible shoes," she said. "Now I'm a national asset. You should have heard my children cheering the President—and the Virgin Islands—at the Inaugural Parade.". . .

The Question of Feminology

"It's a good time to be a woman," said Katie Louchheim who is now a State Department official but has also been—simultaneously and seriatim—a wife, mother, poet, and volunteer in politics and civic affairs.

This sanguine view is not shared by the ladies who habitually write about what one man I know calls "The Woman Bit." Indeed the consensus among them seems to be that the Woman problem has reached crisis proportions, comparable to air pollution and urban sprawl. To distinguish these specialists from the experts who write about fashion, home economics, and child rearing, an enterprising New York newspaper has christened this newer art form Feminology. Journalistically, the field is crowded. But so far as I know, Feminology has not yet been exploited as a parlor game. The possibilities are spectacular.

The object, of course, is to solve the Woman problem, and any number can play. Readers of the women's magazines have been well drilled in the basic gambits. For example: If you live in the city, move to the suburbs; if you live in the suburbs, move to the city; if you are a housewife, get a job; if you have a job, have a baby. And so forth.

Drawing up the rules may prove a bit sticky, since our leading Feminologists are at odds about The Solution. On one side is Phyllis McGinley whose sermons in praise of domesticity, or "nesting" as she calls it, have been packaged in a book called *Sixpence in Her Shoe*. Much as she loves her kitchen, I suspect Miss McGinley (in private life Mrs. Charles Hayden) might be willing to compromise. She is a witty and reasonable woman who writes excellent verse when she finishes her ironing. Indeed, her tone is more soothing than evangelical. She seems less eager to win converts to housewifery than to restore a modicum of tranquillity and better cooking to the homes unsettled by her chief adversary. This is Betty Friedan, high priestess of the "Salvation Through Job" gospel. In the style of Carrie Nation, she flails about at a villain—not the demon rum, but something called *The Feminine Mystique*. This is the title of her book, a shrill, humorless polemic, packed with data mined from the works of psychiatrists, anthropologists and other Feminologists, and interviews with women who are as gabby as they are unhappy.

Naturally, a certain process of self-selection has taken place. Just as an arthritis specialist sees few people who do not have arthritis, Mrs. Friedan specializes in sufferers from what she calls "the problem without a name.". . .

McGinley and Friedan have both made best-sellers of their conflicting theses, which suggests a certain schizophrenia among female book buyers. On the other hand, this odd ambivalence may mean that a good many women are trying to plot a middle course between the two extreme positions, that they are seeking—in the style of Ladybird Johnson—to combine the functions of wife and mother with purposeful work outside their homes, which may or may not involve a professional job.

This posture—which might be called demi-feminism—is by no means a mass movement. The vast majority of American women are not even fractionally feminists and never were. This is why the Suffragists of yore had trouble recruiting doorbell ringers to circulate their petitions and marchers for their parades.

The average woman was otherwise occupied—chiefly in finding a man to support her and thereafter in keeping him reasonably content with his usually tedious job by baking pies and darning his socks when he came home. Such are still the average female's prime concerns.

This fact has been disguised by the tidings that some twenty-three million American women are currently in the "work force" and that three out of five of them are married. This much-touted statistic creates the illusion of a nation of brisk career women who stack the breakfast dishes, park their children in nursery schools, and charge off each morning to "challenging" jobs. . . .

Who then are the twenty-three million? Footnotes to the statistical tables disclose—to those who trouble to read them—that a mere three million are in occupations classed as "technical or professional." Another six million work only intermittently. And most of the remaining fourteen million are in lowly, ill-paid clerical, factory, sales, or service jobs. Of those who are also mothers of young children a dismaying proportion are Negro women. . . .

The Feminologists do not worry much about this female *Lumpenproletariat* [underclass] who, like their male equivalents, are not much given to buying books. . . . The Feminologists' concern is for the Educated Woman, also known as the Trapped Housewife. They find her tormented by doubts as to her worth, plagued by a choice of values and lifestyles, each with its own built-in frustrations.

Women Speak Up

To update my own impressions—which are somewhat different—I decided to confront the Educated Woman in a place where she is currently offered a bewildering variety of choices—Washington, D.C. and its environs. . . .

Eight well-schooled young matrons who live in this area agreed not long ago to spend an evening with me discussing the Woman problem. All were in their early or mid-thirties, mothers of two or more children and married to the same husbands they had started out with. Four were professional women—a doctor, an economist, a teacher, and a biochemist. The rest are listed in the census as "housewives." We spent three delightful hours talking about politics, science, segregation, schools, zoning, mental health, and books. As the last one left to relieve her babysitter I realized to my chagrin that we had not gotten around to the Woman problem though I had made several conscientious attempts to steer the talk in that direction. Apparently no one was greatly interested.

A Demi-Feminist

Realizing that such delicate territory perhaps cannot be probed in a group session, I called next day on one of the housewives who seemed to have a worried look about her. I will call her Jane Jones. "Are you afflicted with the Friedan Syndrome?" I asked.

"I am terribly sorry," she said. "But I don't have time to do much reading outside of my field, which is urban planning. So I have not kept up with all this Feminine Mystique jazz. I have plenty of problems but they all have names. For instance, I am chairman of this committee against discrimination in housing. Some of my best neighbors are bigots. They are also good Democrats and I am Democratic Precinct Chairman. So I have a conflict of roles. . . . So what do I do? Escape mechanism. I bake this absolutely divine Viennese apple cake which the children adore—would you care for a piece?"

The telephone rang at this point and I eavesdropped on a dialogue about setting up a nursery school for culturally deprived children and how to go about getting a subsidy from Operation Head Start (a Poverty War project) to enable their culturally deprived mothers to spend a day a week at the school.

Apologizing for the interruption, Jane returned to our conference and launched into a discourse on what might be called the value system of a demi-feminist. Economically, it has a strong patriarchal base. Jane is convinced that when a man stops bringing home the bacon, marriage collapses. She believes also that marriage—with all its flaws—is the best arrangement yet invented for the rearing of a family.

Since her husband's job is arduous, she feels he is entitled to something better than a TV dinner when he gets home. Besides, she likes cooking. As for his duties as a father? "I don't go for this business of demanding that he change the baby and wash dishes," she said. "I think that's *sick* feminism. Why shouldn't he do something pleasant with the children? And I'd rather have him put up shelves in the basement than putter around my kitchen when he's in a domestic mood. Of course, he baby-sits for me when I'm out working."

The Jones family manages nicely on one salary. So Jane is calm about the fact that she is not paid for her "work."

"I used to laugh at all the Worthy Groups my mother belonged to," she said. "But you know if it weren't for the League of Women Voters our school budget would have been hacked to pieces last year. Honestly, this community would fall apart without us do-gooders and the political parties would collapse.". . .

Jane might be elected to the school board or town council herself next year. But she probably won't try since her husband has had a tempting job offer in the Midwest and may accept. Like the other demi-feminist of her generation she has adapted to the harsh realities of our mobile society. Many factors, of course, are weighed in deciding where the family tent will be pitched—including the quality of schools, the cost of living, and the social and political climate. But in the end what tips the scale is the economic or professional prospect offered the chief breadwinner. Accordingly, Jane has concluded that while the two-job family can work very well (whether or not the wife is paid for her extramural labors), the two-ambition family cannot. Apart from the emotional tension that may be involved, it is not physically feasible for a family to follow two different sets of career opportunities.

Opting for a Limited Career

Thus it is probably geography more than any other factor that accounts for the meager showing of American women in national affairs. What after all, do you do with your husband and family if you are elected to Congress? This handicap is bipartisan. This spring, for example, Patricia Hutar, the capable assistant chairman of the Republican National Committee, gave notice because of what she called her "home situation." The "situation" consisted of a husband and three-year-old daughter in Chicago. She has been replaced by Mary Brooks, a mobile Idaho widow.

Similarly, the Johnson Administration ran into geographic troubles more than a year ago when the President first started looking for women to place in high federal posts. Lists of likely candidates poured in from local political organizations, women's bar associations, and other professional societies.

"But as we started trying to pin individuals down, the lists evaporated," one of the talent scouts told me. "Most women just don't have movable husbands."

Eventually, the search zeroed in on the reservoir of female talent already resident in and around the capital. And in due course some seventy-five executive appointments were made.

But even in Washington the Important Job did not prove an irresistible lure. There was for example a young woman I will call Doris Smith—another demi-feminist. She is a psychologist, the mother of three, and has a part-time job with a private foundation. Why did she turn down the prestige and higher pay the Administration offered her?

"I don't want to be away from home eight hours a day while the children are so young," she said. "And I don't want the kind of high-pressure work that will be on my mind all the time, even when I'm home."

Doris is the daughter of a married career woman of my vintage. She feels she can do a better job with her children than the nannies and fräuleins to whom we entrusted our young. Whether or not this is so, these spinster mercenaries are a vanished breed. And Doris, in any event, says she produced children because she wanted—and enjoys—the experience of rearing them.

So she has opted for the career of limited ambitions. She has equipped herself with a portable vocation that can be practiced wherever her husband (another peripatetic type) decides to hang his professional hat. She is, of course, well aware that a woman who has to pick up the threads of her professional life in a new community every six or seven years—or who withdraws from her field for a decade or more to be a full-time mother—is not going to climb as high as the man who follows his own star or the woman who does not marry.

"But look at the advantages," Doris said. "A husband is insurance against failure—I mean both financial disaster and social stigma. Men are in a much more exposed position. They have to make irrevocable career decisions before they leave college. And if they fail, who will pay off the mortgage?"

As to her own professional prospects. Doris feels rather like a distinguished woman historian I know who was offered a college presidency a few years ago and turned it down because she did not wish to be parted from her husband, a business executive based in a different part of the country. "I can teach or write where we live," she said. "And I really get more fun out of being Jim's wife than I would out of presiding at a faculty council.". . .

In this country, demi-feminism seems to express the established relationship between the sexes, except in those marginal groups where idleness is fashionable or back-breaking toil a necessity.

Changing Opportunities for Women

This pragmatic philosophy will make increasingly good sense as wider opportunities are opened for women to train and perform as full- and part-time professionals and as volunteers, at a pace and on terms suited to their multiple responsibilities. This requires, in the first instance, a realistic assessment of the unfinished business of our society and the role which women could play in getting it done. Little is accomplished toward that end by much of the cant [speech] regularly published about women "as a great wasted national resource.". . .

At the same time, administrators and professionals stubbornly resist the large-scale use of women, either as part-time paid workers or effective volunteers in the very fields where their services are desperately needed—notably the schools, hospitals, social agencies, and libraries.

The programs to which Ladybird Johnson is giving energetic support presage change in this situation. This summer, for example, twenty thousand professional neighborhood, and volunteer workers are to be mobilized to work with preschool children in some three hundred areas. Most of them will be women, and many of them, like Mrs. Johnson, will be chiefly concerned with getting on with the job, cheerfully willing to assume—as the need and circumstances change—the role of wife mother, professional, or volunteer.

What's Going On in the Job Corps

By *U.S. News & World Report*

In his 1965 inaugural address, President Lyndon B. Johnson unveiled his plan to improve the quality of life for all Americans. Known as the "Great Society," President Johnson declared war on poverty and illiteracy and pledged greater aid through federal programs to education, the arts, and housing and urban development. As part of the war on poverty, President Johnson and his administration created the Job Corps, a nationwide organization that placed underprivileged and undereducated young adults into residential programs that provided academic assistance and career training. These programs were designed to take at-risk youth out of neighborhoods where their opportunities for education and advancement were limited because of finance or circumstance. However, less than a year into its development, the program came under fire by citizens of the communities where Job Corps students resided. These citizens complained that Job Corps residents were disrespectful and disruptive to the normal atmosphere of the surrounding communities. In response, *U.S. News & World Report* journalists traveled to Job Corps centers around the country and wrote about the progress of President Johnson's first battle in the war on poverty and the beginning of the Great Society.

At least one phase of President Johnson's "war" on poverty is starting to move. Thousands of youths already are being taken out of slum surroundings—off the streets and into camps.

In the Job Corps for youth, both boys and girls, there will be more than 100,000 enrolled when the plan is in full operation. Here the basic groundwork is expected to be laid so that youths who would be drifting into crime or relief can be trained for useful work.

Of late, the country has been hearing of troubles in the Job Corps.

At a center for girls in St. Petersburg, Fla., eight girls were expelled for drinking. Charges of "rowdyism" were heard.

At a job-training center for boys in Tongue Point, Oreg., a dormitory riot in which lead pipes were hurled led to a one-day suspension of classes.

Stories have been written, too, about the "dropouts" from such centers by dissatisfied youngsters—as many as 30 per cent in some places.

Such reports raised questions about this new venture of Government into youth "rescue" work. To get some answers, staff members of "U.S. News & World Report" visited Job Corps centers for young men from one end of the country to the other.

Unlike CCC

What is taking place, they find, is something entirely new— much different from the Civilian Conservation Corps of the "New Deal" days.

The CCC, begun in a time of deep depression, aimed simply at providing work for jobless male youths, many of whom were college or high-school graduates, not the "dropouts" or unskilled being enrolled into the Job Corps.

Many of the Job Corps boys, aged 16 through 21, are found barely able to read and write. Most are jobless or earning a few dollars a day. All are from poor families and have few prospects for worthwhile careers.

Of the 9,000 young men now in the Corps, the vast majority must go first to "conservation centers," of which 36 have been set up so far.

At these centers, boys are getting basic schooling, along with work and citizenship training in fair play, honesty, the value of a dollar, respect for others and hygiene.

At Toyon, Calif., a dormitory counselor said: "Some of these kids had never used a flush toilet before and didn't know that beds should be made up every day." Camp aides at Fenner Canyon, Calif., write about 30 letters home each week for youngsters, some of whom are not able to write their names or spell the name of their home town. At Camp Catoctin, Md., some boys are being taught how to tell time and how to make a long-distance telephone call.

Many such youngsters are getting treatment for dental and other defects for the first time in their lives. Plentiful food is a new experience for many, and weight gains of 10 pounds in the first month are not uncommon.

Such youngsters, it is found, are in need of help of all kinds. An instructor at Camp Catoctin put it this way:

"About 95 per cent of these boys were lost in the crowd in school. They lost out early and fell further and further behind. They may have been kicked out finally for disciplinary reasons, but the real reason is much deeper.

"Most are 'waiters,' not 'pushers.' They are hesitant to speak—nobody has ever listened to them before."

At the camp in Illinois' Crab Orchard National Wildlife Refuge, a teacher remarked:

"These boys actually want to be told what to do, but we have to be careful when we tell them. You have to have the patience of Job, and discipline has to be flexible."

At this camp, one boy said:

"A big shot from Washington was here the other day, and when he saw the ground around the buildings, he asked us, 'Why ain't the grass in?' So one of the guys here says, 'Whaddya think, we got green thumbs or something?' Some of the guys here ain't used to this kind of work."

Elsewhere, youngsters have sometimes refused to join in body-building exercises or have spurned early-morning muster outside the dormitory.

The "conservation centers" for the least-literate boys are run directly by the Federal Government on federal land.

Emphasis is on bringing them up to eighth-grade achievement levels. But they also are expected to work at such projects as surveying, forestry, fire control, soil-erosion control, building recreational facilities and maintaining roads.

In return, the boys each get $30 per month for spending money—and some of their elected leaders get as much as $50.

Food, shelter, clothing and education are free. In addition, $50 a month is put aside for each boy. If he sends $25 of this to his family, it is matched by the Government.

Youngsters who reach eighth-grade levels—a process that might take a few months to two years—are considered "graduated." Some apply for jobs or join the armed forces or go back to public schools. But many are applying for admission to one of the "urban centers" run by private corporations, State agencies or universities under contract with the Job Corps to provide job training. At such camps, youngsters—at the same rate of pay as that in "conservation centers"—can learn such skills as automobile mechanics, operation and repair of business machines, retail selling, metal trades, electrical work and cooking.

Many of the complaints developing out of the Job Corps program are traced to the drive to enroll 10,000 youngsters by June 30.

At the conservation center in Tillamook, Oreg., reactivation of the naval air base was not completed when the first batch of enrollees arrived.

At Camp Catoctin, staff turnover reached the point where seven different persons held the job of deputy director of education within a six-month period.

At that camp, as at some others, "backlogs" of boys who have finished their basic education are developing. An instructor said:

"Some of our boys are ready to go but are sitting around waiting because 'urban centers' aren't moving fast enough. This is very bad—a few of the boys got tired of waiting and quit. Here again, the Job Corps has been pushing things too fast."

Far more serious are charges of blunders in the recruiting and assigning of youths. Illiterate boys have arrived at basic-education centers expecting to get computer training "like on the posters." On the other hand, a youngster who quit a railroad job to learn electronics found himself in a rural camp in Oregon.

An official at Camp Catoctin reported:

"Local screening of recruits has been very, very bad. One boy came here expecting to be trained as a detective. Others think this is some sort of plush summer camp. We had one pitiful case where you could tell when the boy got off the bus that he never should have passed even the simplest screening. We've had other boys who should have been assigned to job-training centers."

Officials at most camps say that screening procedures seem to have improved in recent weeks—but delays and mix-up still occur.

Antagonism between Corpsmen and nearby townsmen is another worry.

People in Astoria, Oreg., complain about hearing obscene language from Corpsmen at the movie theater. At Marion, Ill., a disturbance began at a rollerskating rink when some Corpsmen showed up with liquor.

Enrollees have not been slow to deliver complaints of their own.

At Crab Orchard, Ill., a Chicago youngster remarked: "Man, I want to get out of here—I don't like that 'Fall Out! Fall Out!' every morning." A Corpsman at an Oregon camp said: "I've been here two months and still not met a girl." At Camp Catoctin, boys complain about "cutting trees and pushing rocks."

Fully Integrated

Job Corps enrollment at present is believed running at about 60 per cent white and 40 per cent Negro. Some camp officials in California said that a few white boys from the South have dropped out rather than live with Negroes. In Tillamook, Oreg., which has no Negro residents of its own, one resident admitted that "we haven't accepted Negroes yet," and barbers are still discussing whether or not they will cut a Negro's hair.

Most boys, however, are adjusting to this problem as well as others.

In a Western camp, a white youngster from Virginia said: "I'd never been with colored people in Virginia, but I've been more friends with them here than with whites."

At Crab Orchard, a Negro who was elected a dormitory leader, had this to say:

"I'm pretty close to some of the white guys. For others, it's hard to see me as a leader—some of them are from the South."

This Negro went on:

"I try to tell all the guys that they better wake up. We're all here in the Job Corps, because we don't know anything yet."

The same view turns up elsewhere. A boy at the Lewiston, Calif., camp said: "No more of this one-way street—going and never coming."

A Georgia boy now at Fenner Canyon explained: "I could

have learned a trade outside, I guess, but I thought the Job Corps would have more patience with me."

Hard at It

Everywhere, camp officials are finding many youngsters pursuing studies with zeal. At Camp Catoctin, an instructor says: "They almost resent my interrupting their studies even though they have worked for two or three hours without looking up from their work."

Boys, too, are learning self-discipline. When a boy at the Toyon, Calif., camp stole a car, the other boys "cut" him socially—and he left quickly. "Self-control" programs are being worked out by elected student leaders at the camps.

Official figures are that 13 per cent of enrollees, nationwide, dropped out. Only 3.2 per cent of those who stayed a month or longer broke away, however. Job Corps policy now is to assign a youngster to a camp far enough from his home to discourage visits which build up his homesickness. Counseling is being stepped up. A Camp Catoctin teacher said:

"I found one boy lying in his bunk crying. He was convinced there was something wrong at home. Finally, we managed to get a call through to his home, and he talked with his mother. This cheered him up. Then, during the week-end, he found a girl friend in a neighboring town, and now he's as happy as a clam here."

Good Community Relations

Strong efforts are being made to build good relations between Corpsmen and residents of nearby towns. Fenner Canyon boys have been invited to join the local softball league, and some of the youngsters at the Kilmer center in New Jersey have been invited to visit in the homes of residents of nearby Edison. One resident gave the Corpsmen the use of his swimming pool.

At the Tongue Point camp, run by the University of Oregon, an official had this comment:

"Two thirds of these kids come from families on relief, some for three and four generations. It's going to take time to undo what 16 to 21 years of living have done to these boys." A California camp director remarked: "If we fail, the alternative for a lot of these guys is jail or a lifetime on relief."

In the fiscal year ending June 30, the Job Corps spent 180 million dollars. Asked from Congress for the fiscal year 1965–1966 is 290 million dollars—out of a total package of 1.5 billion dollars requested for the Office of Economic Opportunity headed by Sargent Shriver.

Not Enough for All

Job Corps officials say this program will not reach all the estimated million youngsters who are eligible. And many of those who do enter the Corps, they add, will fall by the wayside.

Even so, it is being claimed that a success record of 50 per cent would make a sizable dent in the nation's social problems. One Corps official said:

"It's costing maybe a few thousand dollars to give a boy this one last chance to become a solid and useful citizen. If one boy fails, we lost that investment. But for every boy who makes good, we'll be saving the nation the hundreds of thousands of dollars it might have cost to keep him in prison or on relief during a lifetime of failure."

Inside the Watts Riot

By Jerry Cohen and William S. Murphy

Some blamed it on the heat, others on a sad series of misunderstandings, and still others blamed it on a teeming anger that many African Americans felt during the long summer of 1965. Whatever the reason, on August 11 of that year, the Watts community of Los Angeles was ravaged by one of the longest and most violent riots in American history. The rebellion began with a small crowd of passersby who stopped to watch a young male member of the community be arrested for drunk driving and ended in a week of fire, looting, and violence. Police were powerless to stop the attacks on white motorists who passed through the neighborhood, and firemen were routinely stoned as they tried to stop the many cases of arson from spreading. The situation remained out of hand until sixteen thousand National Guard troops were called in to restore order. The riot lasted six days and claimed thirty-four lives, most of whom were black.

One year later, Jerry Cohen and William S. Murphy published *Burn, Baby, Burn*, a compilation of eyewitness narratives from those who experienced the riot firsthand. One of the witnesses, Henry Knawls, was a native Texan and three-year resident of Los Angeles at the time of the Watts rebellion. He tried to "get the pulse of the people whose involvement was so total." Knawls found the pulse of the people by visiting the heart of the rioting community and experiencing for himself the anger, terror, and chaos that fueled the fires of frustration and rebellion for African Americans in Watts and throughout the United States. Although the rebellion took place in Watts, the riots were symptomatic of the racial tension that defined the national mood during that year of protest.

Henry M. Knawls was born in Texas and reared in Portland, Oregon. By the summer of 1965 he had lived in Los Angeles for three years and had been a paid employee of the Neighborhood Youth Corps, an arm of the Economic and Youth Opportunities Agency, since the previous March. He was twenty-five, unmarried and a well-educated and totally dedicated young man. He particularly liked his job specialty: working with high school dropouts in poverty areas and high school graduates experiencing a bitter time while looking for employment.

An ex-serviceman and former student in Northwestern University's school of commerce, Knawls, a Negro, was perplexed at what news media were reporting. Until recently he himself had been a resident of the riot area, and, he recalls: "I didn't believe what I was hearing and seeing on television and reading. I couldn't go along with it."

If it were true, he told himself, he could not condone the rioting. "But I knew their feelings, their frustrations. I've had experiences myself with police. I could see where these people might react violently against policemen," Knawls said.

He still had friends living in the riot area, and he was concerned about them, if what he had been hearing and reading were true. But more important was his growing curiosity about the riot. Shortly after sundown Thursday [August 12] he got into his car and drove south. "I had to get the pulse of these people whose involvement was so total," he remembers thinking.

First Impressions

He arrived in the riot area about 9 P.M., or close to the time of the attack on Ray Fahrenkopf, the television soundman. He left shortly before dawn. So moved was this young Negro man by what he saw and heard and felt, he switched on his tape recorder immediately upon reaching home and dictated this account of his experiences and the observations he made as a result of them:

As I was making a right turn on the street where the action was centered, several Negro youths ran up to my car. They said, "Turn your inside lights on, Blood, so we can see who it is." This I did unquestioningly. I proceeded very slowly up the street, trying to avoid the various sorts of debris, glass, bricks, sticks, by weaving back and forth across the thoroughfare.

Large numbers of men, women and children were gathered on

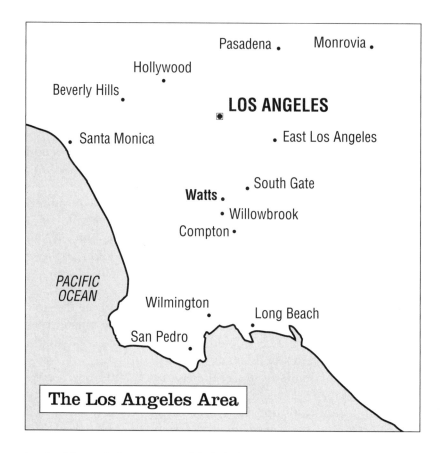

Pasadena • Monrovia •

Hollywood
•

Beverly Hills
•

LOS ANGELES
◙

• Santa Monica   • East Los Angeles

• South Gate
Watts •
• Willowbrook
Compton •

PACIFIC
OCEAN   Wilmington
•
Long Beach
San Pedro •
•

The Los Angeles Area

both sides of the street with bricks and other objects in their hands. Just up the street was a car which had been upturned and set afire. From their comments, "We gon' mess over some devils," "Don't let no gray boys get through here," and "Paddies better stay out of here tonight," one could assume that they were anxiously waiting any car with white occupants to come driving down the street.

After driving back down the street and parking my car, I mingled with the crowd. At just about this time a car came roaring down the street. The crowd yelled: "Whitey! Get him!"

Bricks, stone and pipes, hurled from both sides of the street, dented both sides of the car. The front windshield was smashed. The car speeded up and kept going until it was out of the area. People screamed: "Don't let no more get away." And: "Dammit, they got through." They were disappointed that they had not been able to stop this car and inflict more damage upon it and its driver.

Down the street was heard: "We got him, we got one." I ran up the street with several people and saw a Caucasian man being pulled from his car. One group began pummeling the man, and others proceeded to overturn his car and put a torch to it. The man was allowed to run away after he had been thoroughly beaten; he could run only with a stumbling gait and both hands were covering his bloody face.

Police Turned Back

Several police cars came driving down this street and were stoned with missiles from both sides of the street. The police did not stop, but made U-turns and headed back the way they had come. I proceeded up the street for two or three blocks, and across the street, at a gas station, approximately nine or ten police cars were forming a semicircle in front of the station. The policemen were crouched down behind their cars with their pistols and rifles drawn and aimed at the crowd facing them. The police made no attempts to disperse the crowd, which was continually taunting the officers to shoot, and calling them names.

After about fifteen minutes, all of these policemen got into their cars and left, with red lights flashing and sirens screaming. They went down the street toward the area where the riot supposedly started. They were bombarded with missiles as they sped down the street.

Another car with a Caucasian driver came cruising down the street, much slower than the first one. The people rushed into the street in front of the car, forcing it to stop. The driver jumped out of the car before he could be pulled out. In his hand was a .45-caliber automatic pistol.

He did not fire the gun, but, instead, started running down the street. The crowd pursued and finally caught him, took the gun away and began beating him. His car also was turned over and set afire.

The people around, watching the man being beaten, kept yelling: "Beat that——. Teach him to keep his ass out of Watts."

A brick came out of nowhere and smashed through the window of a hot dog stand across the street.

Looting

Someone yelled: "That's Whitey's, tear it down." A number of people from both sides of the street converged on the stand and began breaking all the windows. Several men climbed into this stand and began passing out Cokes and other beverages to the people outside.

After they had completely depleted the stock of wieners, Cokes and everything else of value that could be carried out, they evacuated the stand and began walking down the street toward a couple of stores. They did not set fire to this stand.

As they passed a small gas station, several people wanted to set it afire. One of the people standing nearby the station told them: "Let it stand. Blood owns it."

A liquor store and grocery store were the next targets. First, the windows were knocked in. Then the people poured into the stores—men, women, children. They rushed back and forth, in and out, carrying as much as they could: groceries, liquor and cigarettes.

Two police cars came roaring down the street and pulled up in front of the store. The people inside came rushing out and ran right by the policemen who made no attempt to stop or apprehend them. The police got out of their cars and set up a temporary blockade in front of the store with their rifles pointed toward the crowd across the street. They remained there for approximately fifteen minutes and left. Before they had gotten a half a block away, the looting resumed.

Next door to the liquor store was a meat market. These windows also were smashed and people in cars drove up and began loading meat into the trunks of their cars. Two young boys (they looked to be nine or ten years old) came running out of the store and across the street carrying a side of beef. The crowd roared its approval and greeted the boys with laughter and cheers.

Several men came walking toward me laden down with liquor. One of them paused in front of me and asked: "What do you drink, brother?" He and the other stopped right there on the street to have a drink. My reply was: "Whiskey."

They opened a bottle of whiskey and handed it to me. I drank a large swallow and handed it back. Twice around and the bottle was empty. We laughed and they continued down the street. Looking back the way I had come, there was another burning car which had been turned over.

A cry went up the street: "One-Oh-Three. Hit the Third!" It referred to 103rd Street, the business center of Watts (a mile to the east and the north). The people piled into cars and headed for

103rd Street. Others followed on foot. As I was getting back into my car to drive to "One-Oh-Three," several men jumped into my car and said: "Let's make it, baby."

After parking the car approximately a half-block off 103rd on a side street, we all piled out and separated when we reached the main street (Central Avenue). A few hundred people had already arrived.

The iron gratings in front of the stores and businesses were forced first. Then the windows broke. Dozens of people climbed in and out of the stores with armloads of clothing, appliances, guns and liquor.

There were three squad cars that went back and forth on 103rd. The policemen made no attempt to get out of them and stop the looting. However, the people would run out of the stores just as the police cars approached the business area and hide in the alleys or behind the stores.

As soon as the cars had passed the looting would continue. Walking back and forth on both sides of the street, I paused at a pawnshop and observed several people coming out with portable TVs, record players, sewing machines and clothes.

One man came out with a stereo console on his back.

A youth who looked to be about thirteen or fourteen years old came running out with four or five rifles in his arms.

Suddenly, someone yelled: "The fuzz." A Negro woman came rushing out with two portable TV sets. She was unable to move freely with both sets, and as she was coming out, she asked me: "You want one of these?"

I replied: "I ain't got no place to put it, baby."

She dropped one of the sets on the sidewalk and ran off into the night.

Every Burglar Alarm Ringing

The police cars slowly passed the pawnshop and kept going. I walked back up the street and stopped in front of a large department store.

The metal grating had been pulled up from the street and a large window had been smashed. People were rushing in and out with armloads of clothing. A yell went out that the police were coming back.

Some of the looting crowd ran out and behind the store, but just as many simply crouched behind the counters in the store.

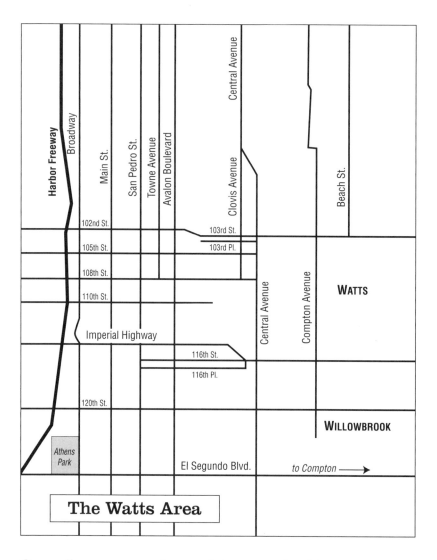

The Watts Area

One police car swerved around the corner by this store.

A very young Negro boy was picking up a case of cuff links someone had dropped. A policeman roared: "Put that down."

The boy quickly dropped the case and walked away. The squad car pulled around and continued down 103rd. A crowd converged on the store as soon as the police left.

No buildings were set afire. Every burglar alarm on this street was ringing, however. I walked across the street and stood in front of a laundromat. Four of the police cars parked about fifty feet away and the policemen got out and started walking toward me. There were four city policemen and four county (deputy sheriffs) or state (Highway Patrol) policemen. They came up to me and asked, not too courteously: "What the hell are you doing on the street?"

Before I could answer, a heavyset Negro woman who had been in the laundromat answered: "He's washing,———. Is that all right?"

The officer replied: "Well, get off the street and stay off the street."

The woman stood very defiantly in front of them and made no move to go back inside the laundromat. The policemen looked menacingly at her and then at me. They turned and walked back to their cars.

Turning around, I saw approximately fourteen Negro people who had been inside the laundromat now standing in the doorway.

Had the policemen made any attempt to take into custody the Negro woman or me, I feel reasonably sure that there would have been an incident.

The Negro woman who had come to my defense then cautioned me: "Listen, baby, don't put your hands in your pocket like that when they're talkin' to you. They'll burn you in a minute."

I thanked her and walked into the laundromat with her and talked for several minutes. She expressed concern over the people who had been, and were going to be, hurt in this thing. But she felt that maybe this would make them, the police, stop treating the people like dogs because now people would stand up to them.

"Burn, Baby, Burn"

While walking back to my car, I saw someone throw a brick through the rear window of my car. I ran up to the car and the young men around me asked if it was mine. I said it was.

They told me I should have parked farther down the street and that they didn't know it belonged to a "Blood." They helped me clear away the glass and I drove off.

Driving back up 103rd Street, I watched a car pull up in front of a store. I recognized two of the men as residents of an area far removed from Watts. In fact, they lived in what is regarded as a middle-income Negro area.

Then, I was stopped by a police roadblock as I was leaving the area, told to get out of the car, searched and allowed to proceed.

As I drove through the predominantly Negro-inhabited central section of Los Angeles, I saw only one other incident, a car with white occupants speeding through a barrage of rocks and sticks.

The car was approximately a block and a half in front of me. After it had passed the crowd, the people turned toward my car. I turned my inside lights on, slowed down, honked my horn and yelled out the window: "Burn, baby, burn."

Some of these people echoed my words. And I was allowed to pass by unmolested. From 103rd Street down to Adams Boulevard (approximately 26th Street) there were large numbers of Negroes congregated on porches, in parked cars and just standing along the curb, even at this early hour of the morning.

A Bond with These People

It was then about 2 A.M. Most of these people had nothing in their hands. But it seemed to me they were just waiting. Three observations remained keen in my mind:

One—The involvement of the community: those not actually throwing stones or looting appeared to be in favor of those who were. Both older men and women, and young boys and girls, were committing overt acts of hostility.

Two—The widespread hatred throughout the rioting Negro community of [Police] Chief Parker; at one period several groups were chanting: "Send Parker out here."

Three—No community leaders were apparent, making attempts to calm or halt the mobs. It is my opinion that this would have been an ineffectual gesture anyway. The mobs throughout the area seemed to be of one mind in striking out against the police, and Caucasians in general.

I did not feel like an outsider at any time during the night. While my involvement was passive, and some of the sights I witnessed appalling and saddening, I felt a strong bond with these people.

The Delano Grape Strikes

By Cesar Chavez

Though the only clear war zones were those in Vietnam, 1965 seemed to be a year of battles in which U.S. citizens from varying social classes, ethnicities, and regions were engaged in the common struggle for equality and justice. In California, a continuing confrontation between migrant farmworkers and the owners of the land they cultivated turned grapes into a point of serious contention and revolution. With the dissolution of Public Law 78 of the U.S. Congress in 1951, braceros, or Mexican laborers who legally entered the southwestern United States in order to harvest large farms, were no longer allowed legal passage into the country. The end of government-sanctioned bracero labor resulted in a backlash of low wages and unfair treatment for those laborers who did have legal residency.

Cesar Chavez represented the National Farm Workers Association (NFWA), a union for Hispanic American farmworkers. The NFWA and other grassroots organizations were scarcely organized and hardly poised for the arduous strikes against the large-scale farming industry that began in September 1965. Despite strong opposition and poor support from those who did agree with the NFWA, Chavez, along with other migrant union organizers, led one of the largest and most successful labor strikes in U.S. history. Chavez called for a peaceful, organized strike in protest against the poor wages and living conditions of the farmworkers. However, in connection with the high tensions that seized the entire country in that year of protest, many of the strikes in-

Jacques E. Levy, *Cesar Chavez: Autobiography of La Causa*. New York: W.W. Norton, 1975.

volved violence and arrest. Furthermore, the victory was not immediate. Growers did not concede to union demands until 1970, five years after picketing began.

Recorded by writer Jacques E. Levy, Cesar Chavez tells of the tension and victory of the Delano grape strikes in his own words. Levy began working as a reporter for the *Press Democrat* in Santa Rosa, California, in 1957, where he witnessed the continuing plight of the farmworkers. After collaborating for some time with Cesar Chavez on the 1975 book *Cesar Chavez: Autobiography of La Causa*, Levy eventually quit his job with the *Press Democrat* and devoted himself to writing the story of Cesar Chavez and the labor struggle in California.

I found out about the grape strike on September 8, 1965, when Manuel Uranday, his wife Esther, and his father came to the office to tell me the Filipinos were on strike.
"Oh, no!" I said.
"What are we going to do?"
"Well, we can't call a strike, because we have to take a vote," I said after we discussed what was happening.

I learned that Filipino workers from a camp at Lucas and Sons had stopped work, and the strike had spread quickly to other growers. Earlier that summer, AWOC [Agricultural Workers Organizing Committee] had struck in Thermal in the Coachella Valley because the pay was below $1.40 an hour, the prevailing wage for braceros in the Imperial Valley south of Coachella. Actually the bracero law had expired in 1964, but Governor Pat Brown had persuaded Secretary of Labor Willard Wirtz to allow braceros into California at that wage rate. Since growers weren't using braceros in the Coachella Valley, they dropped the wage to $1.10 for Chicano grape pickers and $1.25 for the Filipinos. AWOC called a strike, and in ten days the pay was raised. But AWOC didn't get a contract. . . .

We quickly had a board meeting, discussed the situation, and pretty much decided that this was it. I said it was going to be a long struggle, and the only way we could win was by staying with it. I said that our job was not to get discouraged if we went up like a wave and then came down, that at the point that we came down, we would start with whatever we had left.

We talked about the need to make the strike a public controversy as soon as possible to get it out of the Delano area, not letting the growers choke it there, but publicizing it. I was sure we couldn't win it by ourselves. We needed money. And in order for the growers to come out with what they really thought of Unions, the best way was to put them under pressure and let them express themselves to the public.

Preparing to Strike

We decided to drop everything and start organizing for a mass meeting to get a good strike vote. Well, I was using this for organizing, too. I wanted to have the meeting on September 16, Mexican Independence Day, the great Mexican holiday marking the end of Spanish rule.

There was much to do, finding a meeting place, getting all the members there, and preparing a case for us with the growers, AWOC, and the public. We put out different leaflets every day going door to door in Delano, McFarland, Richgrove, Earlymart, parts of Wasco, Porterville, and Bakersfield. . . .

During that first week, the strike spread to about two thousand workers and some twenty farm labor camps. In some places the growers locked the workers out of the camps, camps where they had been living for years. In others, the men refused to leave, and the utilities were shut off. Then the growers added armed security guards, one of whom took a shot at a striker.

So there was a lot of excitement by the time we held our meeting. The hall at Our Lady of Guadalupe Church in Delano was large and had a balcony. We had put up our huge Union flag and posters of Zapata [a leader of the Mexican revolution] and Jack London's "Definition of a Strike Breaker." By the time the meeting started, the hall and balcony were jam-packed, and people were coming out of the rafters.

There were guys from every ranch in the area. We made sure of that so, when a strike vote was taken, it would be a general strike of all growers. The meeting was very spirited, a band played, and every so often the hall rang out with cries of "Viva La Causa!"

We first talked about the Filipino brothers, about solidarity and the need to have a general strike. When my turn came, I recalled a little history.

"155 years ago in the state of Guanajuato in Mexico," I said, "a padre proclaimed the struggle for liberty. He was killed, but ten years later Mexico won its independence." And then I spoke of the present. "We are engaged in another struggle for the freedom and dignity which poverty denies us. But it must not be a violent struggle, even if violence is used against us. Violence can only hurt us and our cause.

"The strike was begun by the Filipinos, but it is not exclusively for them," I said. "Tonight we must decide if we are to join our fellow workers in this great labor struggle.". . .

Before the meeting ended, we voted to have the same demands as AWOC, $1.40 an hour, 25 cents a box, and $12 a gondola.

Then I made a final appeal to keep the strike nonviolent. "Are you in agreement?" I asked.

"Si!" they roared back.

After the strike vote, I asked for several days to try to get the growers to meet with us. I wanted to prepare a case so that if we went to the public, they'd know we tried to meet with the growers. It was also hoping against hope. We knew the growers weren't going to meet with us, but we were hoping that somehow they would. . . .

Facing the Opposition

We were up before dawn Monday morning. Before the day was over, more than twelve hundred workers had joined the strike in an area covering about four hundred square miles of vineyards.

There was a lot of excitement, a lot of optimism, and a tremendous amount of activity. In those days we didn't know how to organize the people for maximum production, and there was a lot of wasted effort, a lot of people constantly coming and going.

Our office was a little store at the corner of First and Albany, no bigger than 20 by 40 feet, and it was jam-packed. We used it as an office, as a service center, as a dormitory, and as a meeting hall. We never closed. And we were picketing every day, getting up very early each morning and going to bed very late at night.

Ironically, although in the Mexican custom the man is really the boss of the house, once the strike started, women became freer quicker than the men. And it's been our experience everywhere since then. The women are not afraid. They know what they're doing because it means beans and shoes for their kids.

Sometimes pickets asked, "What's the use of picketing?" because they were picketing and couldn't even see the people working deep in the vineyards. The answer was that they affected production.

"Just keep talking to the scabs," I said [scabs are those who worked in spite of the picket]. "After a while, if it's done the right way, they begin to leave. Somebody else may take their place, or it looks like the job is filled, but it isn't really. There's a loss of time. The grower is getting people who are not experienced, who have never seen grapes in their lives. For the employer that's loss of money."

"We've got to make the grower spend fifty dollars to our one dollar," I said. "We affect production and costs and profit. And if we hold out, we can win."

In addition, to me the picket line is something very special. Unless you have been on a picket line, you just can't understand the feeling you get there, seeing the conflict at its two most acid ends. It's a confrontation that's vivid. It's a real education.

Without knowing it, the workers also had more than just a picket line; they had the nerve to be in a picket line and to be striking.

The growers were very angry at the challenge. How dare they strike the bosses! Both surprised and hurt, they struck back. On the first day, I left two workers to picket the entrance of a ranch near the office. A short time later they were back, breathless.

"What happened?" I asked. "Where's your car?" They had run about a mile to the office.

They said a grower had pointed a shotgun at them and threatened to kill them. He grabbed their picket signs, set them on fire, and when they didn't burn fast enough, he blasted the signs with his shotgun.

The incident was reported to the police, but nothing happened.

A few days later, when we had about six or seven pickets in front of a labor contractor's home, about twenty or thirty growers came over there half-drunk from a party. Julio Hernandez ran to tell me that the growers had beaten one of our men. So I went over and got on the picket line.

The growers were giving us the knee and the elbow, knocking us down and throwing us down. But we remained nonviolent. We weren't afraid of them. We just got up and continued picketing.

A big crowd started forming, booing the growers. Then the Filipinos, who were having a meeting in Filipino Hall, got in their cars and raced over. The growers suddenly were surrounded by angry people. Police, sheriff's deputies, and the fire department arrived.

One of the growers started getting rough with one of the cops, who put him in his patrol car, handcuffed him, and drove him to jail. There they released him. When we finally left, we were bruised, and I had sore ribs and legs and back for a while. Nothing happened to the growers.

As days passed, there was more violence. Growers pushed people around on the picket lines, ran tractors between pickets and the field to cover them with dust and dirt, and drove cars and pickups with guns and dogs dangerously close to pickets at high speeds.

One day, when Episcopal Bishop Sumner Waiters joined our pickets, he was a victim of one of those dust attacks. Later, one grower used his sulphur rig to spray the pickets. When he finally was tried, he was acquitted. . . .

A Seesaw Battle

During the first days of the strike things looked very good—as they usually do—then about the sixth day, did they look bad. From then on it was a seesaw battle.

There were days when we got all kinds of strikebreakers out of the fields. On others we didn't. At times they'd almost drive us out, and we'd regroup our strength and come back again. Sometimes we couldn't even go picketing because there were so many [legal] injunctions. We could hardly move. Other times we weren't picketing because we didn't have any gas for the cars—we didn't have any money at all. Our guys went for about six months without getting a bill paid for anything. And we were discouraged.

More than once the authorities threatened to close our office down. Some of the people that were sent to do a job on us obviously didn't like it at all. I don't remember who it was, but I think it was the fire marshal who hated the politics of his assignment and told us so on more than one occasion. But they kept up their investigations under the health and building codes and the fire code. They were just on the verge of knocking us completely out, but we lucked out.

There was constant intimidation and harassment. Every single person who came to our office had his license plate number taken down. If he went to town, he would be stopped and questioned.

Of course, after a while, we welcomed this because every time the cops stopped these people, they'd get madder and help us more. . . .

One of the first jobs we had to do was to get our people conditioned, so they wouldn't be afraid of the police. If they're not afraid, then they can keep a lot of things cool, but the moment they're uncertain, then anything can happen.

There was other harassment on the picket lines. At one point, after we had been on strike for about five or six weeks, we were stopped constantly by deputies. Every striker was photographed, and a field-report card was filled in on each person. In some cases, it took as much as an hour and a half to go through this process. Then it was repeated every time we moved from one field to another. We have a man in Delano who was photographed, and the same report was filled in on him no less than twelve times.

At first our tactic was total cooperation. Then we started taking their time. In my case, the officer took almost an hour because I went very slowly. I examined the card and the spelling, and I engaged in conversation just to tie him up.

Then we'd go on night picketing, get about thirty cars and go out at night, and they'd have to wake up the cops to follow us. We worked it so they had to have three shifts. If we'd go out of the office at 3:00 in the morning, they'd follow us.

With us, it was a tactic to get them to spend as much money as possible. The county spent thousands of dollars on extra personnel. They'll never spend that much money again. Afterward there were a lot of complaints. A small group of liberals in Bakersfield checked up on the expense and found they had spent thousands of dollars.

Finally we made up our minds we had been harassed enough. We refused to give them any information or to let them take our pictures. We told the inquiring officer from the Kern County Sheriff's Office that if he wanted more information from us or wanted to take our picture, he would first have to arrest us. And at that point we were able to gain some ground.

We found that the opposition has a certain way of responding, a very typical way of responding. That was the case with the growers, but it could be with any opposition. It goes through predictable stages, and they all happened to us.

At the first stage, they ignore us. That happened at the beginning of the Movement when I was running around trying to get it going. Then they ridicule us. People say, "Oh, he's crazy." Next comes the repression. Eventually—after a long time—comes the respect. . . .

A Clever Plan to Incite Support

Since I was scheduled to speak . . . on the steps of Sproul Hall at the University of California in Berkeley, we decided to have all our volunteer pickets arrested early in the morning, so that by the time I got to Berkeley, I could make the announcement. This was just a year after the big Free Speech fights there, and the students were politically militant.

Well, the pickets went out to the W.B. Camp ranch, spotted a crew, and started hollering "Huelga! Huelga! Huelga!"—"Strike! Strike! Strike!"—at the scabs. When [a police officer] ordered them to stop, they ignored his command and continued shouting. All were arrested. . . .

Wendy Goepel, a volunteer, drove me that day to Berkeley in a little Volkswagen. After I talked about the strike, I made the announcement of the forty-four arrested just for shouting "Huelga" out in the vineyards, and I asked the students to give me their lunch money for the strikers. It was a big rally, and the response was great.

I had other speaking engagements that day at San Francisco State College, Mills, and Stanford. . . .

Besides [monetary support] we got a lot of press, and then, of course, I attacked the sheriffs department bitterly, asking the students to send letters and telegrams and make phone calls to the sheriff.

For about three days the forty-four strikers stayed in jail while [the union staged] . . . demonstrations and pray-ins in front of the jail. We applied a lot of pressure. . . .

The Grape Boycott

We started the grape boycott helter skelter in October 1965, about a month after the [main] strike started. We had to organize the people first, so they could be more effective and more disciplined. Then, in November, we started putting picket lines wherever the grapes went. We began to send the people to San Francisco and Los Angeles and to have them follow the truckloads of grapes.

When we set up a picket line at one of the piers in San Francisco, all the longshoremen walked out. They, of course, wouldn't go to work unless we left. So we got the ILWU (International Longshoremen's and Warehousemen's Union) in trouble, but they wouldn't tell us to leave. . . .

Three months later, when the strike had been going on six

months, we got more major national publicity. Senator Harrison Williams's Subcommittee on Migratory Labor came to California for three days of hearings, one in Sacramento, one in San Francisco, and one in Delano. They wanted to have it in Fresno, but we fought with them to have it in Delano.

At first Senator Robert Kennedy wasn't going to come, but we wanted him, and he finally agreed. He came for the last hearing in Delano, and that was great, especially when he recognized our Union and came to speak at our meeting.

Shortly before the subcommittee came, about twenty or thirty of our pickets were arrested when scabs threatened to harm them. Our peaceful pickets were arrested instead of the scabs who threatened them. We gave Kennedy that bit of information, and he began to question the old sheriff, Leroy Galyen, who had been elected sheriff way back in 1954. . . . Galyen was an old captain of the California Highway Patrol.

"What did you arrest them for?" Senator Kennedy asked.

"Well, if I have reason to believe that there's going to be a riot started, and somebody tells me that there's going to be trouble if you don't stop them, it's my duty to stop them."

Kennedy asked the sheriff, "Who told you that they're going to riot?"

"The men right out in the field that they were talking to said, 'If you don't get them out of here, we're going to cut their hearts out.' So rather than let them get out, we removed the cause," the sheriff said. . . .

Finally, as Senator Williams called a lunch recess, Senator Kennedy said firmly, "Can I suggest that in the interim period of time, the luncheon period of time, that the sheriff and the district attorney read the Constitution of the United States?"

ARTICLE 13

Unsafe at Any Speed

By Ralph Nader

In 1965 the automobile was just over fifty years old. In those five decades, the automobile evolved from the slow-moving Model T into the speedy, aerodynamically designed muscle car of the 1960s. With the growing power and speed, Americans discovered that the marvels of mass transportation also introduced alarmingly high accident and death rates. In response to the growing concern over automobile fatalities, author and politician Ralph Nader wrote *Unsafe at Any Speed*, a book that examined the danger of automobiles and the automotive industry. In the preface to his book, Nader explained that highway accidents alone supported an entire service industry devoted to assisting injured drivers and cleaning up the aftermath. Nader's concern, as presented in the preface and then reiterated throughout his book, was that not enough preventative measures were being taken to eliminate highway accidents and educate automobile owners about safe driving. He wanted the automobile industry to be accountable to legislation aimed at improving safety.

For over half a century the automobile has brought death, injury, and the most inestimable sorrow and deprivation to millions of people. With Medea-like intensity, this mass trauma began rising sharply four years ago reflecting new and unexpected ravages by the motor vehicle. A 1959 Department of Commerce report projected that 51,000 persons would be killed by automobiles in 1975. That figure will probably be reached in 1965, a decade ahead of schedule.

A transportation specialist, Wilfred Owen, wrote in 1946, "There is little question that the public will not tolerate for long an annual traffic toll of forty to fifty thousand fatalities." Time has shown Owen to be wrong. Unlike aviation, marine, or rail transportation, the highway transport system can inflict tremendous casualties and property damage without in the least affecting the viability of the system. Plane crashes, for example, jeopardize the attraction of flying for potential passengers and therefore strike at the heart of the air transport economy. They motivate preventative efforts. The situation is different on the roads.

The Cost of Carnage

Highway accidents were estimated to have cost this country in 1964, $8.3 billion in property damage, medical expenses, lost wages, and insurance overhead expenses. Add an equivalent sum to comprise roughly the indirect costs and the total amounts to over two per cent of the gross national product. But these are not the kind of costs which fall on the builders of motor vehicles (excepting a few successful law suits for negligent construction of the vehicle) and thus do not pinch the proper foot. Instead, the costs fall to users of vehicles, who are in no position to dictate safer automobile designs.

In fact, the gigantic costs of the highway carnage in this country support a service industry. A vast array of services—medical, police, administrative, legal, insurance, automotive repair, and funeral—stand equipped to handle the direct and indirect consequences of accident injuries. Traffic accidents create economic demands for these services running into billions of dollars. It is in the post-accident response that lawyers and physicians and other specialists labor. This is where the remuneration lies and this is where the talent and energies go. Working in the area of prevention of these casualties earns few fees. Consequently our society has an intricate organization to handle direct and indirect aftermaths of collisions. But the true mark of a humane society must be what it does about *prevention* of accident injuries, not the cleaning up of them afterward.

A Duty to Promote Safety

Unfortunately, there is little in the dynamics of the automobile industry that works for its reduction. Doctors, lawyers, engineers and other specialists have failed in their primary professional ethic: to dedicate themselves to the prevention of accident-injuries. The roots of the unsafe vehicle problem are so entrenched that the situation can be improved only by the forging of new instruments of citizen action. When thirty practicing physicians picketed for safe auto design at the New York International Automobile Show on April 7, 1965, their unprecedented action was the measure of their desperation over the inaction of the men and institutions in government and industry who have failed to provide the public with the vehicle safety to which it is entitled. The picketing surgeons, orthopedists, pediatricians and general practitioners marched in protest because the existing medical, legal and engineering organizations have defaulted.

A great problem of contemporary life is how to control the power of economic interests which ignore the harmful effects of their applied science and technology. The automobile tragedy is one of the most serious of these man-made assaults on the human body. The history of that tragedy reveals many obstacles which must be overcome in the taming of any mechanical or biological hazard which is a by-product of industry or commerce. Our society's obligation to protect the "body rights" of its citizens with vigorous resolve and ample resources requires the precise, authoritative articulation and front-rank support which is being devoted to civil rights.

This country has not been entirely laggard in defining values relevant to new contexts of a technology laden with risks. The postwar years have witnessed a historic broadening, at least in the courts, of the procedural and substantive rights of the injured and the duties of manufacturers to produce a safe product. Judicial decisions throughout the fifty states have given living meaning to Walt Whitman's dictum, "If anything is sacred, the human body is sacred." Mr. Justice Jackson in 1953 defined the duty of the manufacturers by saying, "Where experiment or research is necessary to determine the presence or the degree of danger, the product must not be tried out on the public, nor must the public be expected to possess the facilities or the technical knowledge to learn for itself of inherent but latent dangers. The claim that a hazard was not foreseen is not available to one who did not use foresight appropriate to his enterprise."

It is a lag of almost paralytic proportions that these values of safety concerning consumers and economic enterprises, reiterated many times by the judicial branch of government, have not found their way into legislative policy-making for safer automobiles. Decades ago legislation was passed, changing the pattern of private business investments to accommodate more fully the safety value on railroads, in factories, and more recently on ships and aircraft. In transport, apart from the motor vehicle, considerable progress has been made in recognizing the physical integrity of the individual. There was the period when railroad workers were killed by the thousands and the editor of *Harper's* could say late in the last century: "So long as brakes cost more than trainmen, we may expect the present sacrificial method of car-coupling to be continued." But injured trainmen did cause the railroads some operating dislocations; highway victims cost the automobile companies next to nothing and the companies are not obliged to make use of developments in science-technology that have demonstrably opened up opportunities for far greater safety than any existing safety features lying unused on the automobile companies' shelves.

A principal reason why the automobile has remained the only transportation vehicle to escape being called to meaningful public account is that the public has never been supplied the information nor offered the quality of competition to enable it to make effective demands through the marketplace and through government for a safe, nonpolluting and efficient automobile that can be produced economically. The consumer's expectations regarding automotive innovations have been deliberately held low and mostly oriented to very gradual annual style changes. The specialists and researchers outside the industry who could have provided the leadership to stimulate this flow of information by and large chose to remain silent, as did government officials.

The persistence of the automobile's immunity over the years has nourished the continuance of that immunity, recalling Francis Bacon's insight: "He that will not apply new remedies must expect new evils, for time is the greatest innovator."

The accumulated power of decades of effort by the automobile industry to strengthen its control over car design is reflected today in the difficulty of even beginning to bring it to justice. The time has not come to discipline the automobile for safety; that time came over four decades ago. But that is not cause to delay any longer what should have been accomplished in the nineteen-twenties.

The Longest Night

By Elliott Osborn

Just as the evening commute was beginning to intensify along the northeastern seaboard on a Tuesday night in November, the lights went out. Not just the lights of a few houses and businesses or even a few neighborhoods, but the lights of several large metropolitan cities in several states. Linked by a web of power lines and circuits, these cities were mysteriously cut off from their power supply, and in some places they were cut off for the entire night. Due to the events of that unstable year, including the uneasy fear of Cold War enemies, the battle against communism in Vietnam, and the rioting and looting that had rocked the nation, a long night with no power or communication could have resulted in chaos. Those who were trapped in the blackness did not know how or why the power was out, they only knew that they were trapped, some in subways, in offices, or in elevators, without power. *Newsweek* editor Elliott Osborn included the reactions of people from Massachusetts to Manhattan in the magazine's report on the power outage. When Osborn, a renowned newspaperman, once said that "journalistic hours are odd and long and often tense" he no doubt referred to such times as that long Tuesday night in November when all the lights went out.

T he northeastern U.S. is the Megalopolis—a vast intermeshing of cities, towns, suburbs and exurbs. It is urban America of the mid–twentieth century brought to its fullest flower—and its fullest fragility. It is utterly dependent on turbine technology—a world that runs on electricity and on the faith that one has only to push a button, flick a switch or throw a lever to make electricity work. Electricity is its pulse, its power, its *élan vital*. And then one night last week the electricity stopped.

At 5:17 P.M. in Buffalo, 5:17 in Rochester, 5:18 in Boston, 5:28 in Albany, 5:24 to 5:28 in New York City, the clocks in the Megalopolis sputtered to a standstill. Lights blinked and dimmed and went out. Skyscrapers towered black against a cold November sky, mere artifacts lit only by the moon. Elevators hung immobile in their shafts. Subways ground dead in their tunnels. Streetcars froze in their tracks. Street lights and traffic signals went out— and with them the best-laid plans of the traffic engineers. Airports shut down. Mail stacked up in blacked-out post offices. Computers lost their memories. TV pictures darkened and died. Business stopped. Food started souring in refrigerators. Telephones functioned but dial tones turned to shrill whines under a record overload. Nothing else seemed to work except transistor radios—and radios could only share the puzzlement and finally deliver the comforting news that the world had not come to an end, that the blackout was neither the judgment of God nor an Armageddon with the Communists, that almost the entire Northeast had simply fallen victim to its very dependence on The System.

Cascade

The System, in this case, was the sprawling, interconnected grid of power networks that girdle the region—and when The System mysteriously broke down, the result was the most colossal power failure in history. It was a breakdown that wasn't supposed to have happened; only a year before, a Federal Power Commission report had pronounced such grids relatively invulnerable even to nuclear attack. But happen it did, and, if the immediate cause remained elusive for days afterward, the effect did not. Like a string of Christmas-tree lights, one power system after another blinked out in a wave of failures cascading down from the upper reaches of the grid. The big blackout swept across Upstate New York and southern Canada, raced across most of New England, turned off four of New York City's five boroughs, dimmed lights momentarily as far north as Maine and as far south as Washington.

At its peak, the power failure was simply beyond human scale: it engulfed 80,000 square miles across parts of eight U.S. states and Canada's Ontario province—and left 30 million people in the dark. Whole cities were reduced to cold, black outcroppings in an inky landscape—Buffalo for 40 minutes, Rochester for four hours, Syracuse for 40 minutes, Albany for four hours, Toronto for four hours in three bursts, Providence for two and a half hours, Boston for five and a half hours.

The Most

In all the Megalopolis, New York was the biggest city—and so, naturally, all its problems were multiplied by the density of its population, the height of its towers, the length of its subway tunnels. New York's blackout was the longest—more than thirteen hours in some parts. It affected the most people—600,000 trapped in stalled subways, nearly 100,000 stranded waiting for commuter trains that never ran, numberless hundreds caged in elevators, numberless thousands penned in their skyscraper aeries. New York's losses were the most staggering: $100 million, by one estimate, in undone business alone. And New York's recovery was the slowest; it took two days to nurse the patient back to normal.

Incredibly, the blackout stopped short of catastrophe. The lost story of the longest night lay, indeed, in what *didn't* happen: there were no plane crashes, no train wrecks, no disastrous fires, no crime waves or looting sprees. And there was no panic. All across the Megalopolis, the cliff dwellers—who had come to believe in their own folk image as so many encapsulated, private atoms—surprised themselves with their neighborly good spirit at an hour when everyone, at last, had something in common.

Yet what they had in common was nonetheless, while it lasted, an authentic national emergency in everything but name—and it lacked the name chiefly because the U.S. Office of Emergency Planning feared that proclaiming it might indeed set off a panic. Lyndon Johnson heard the news via car radio while motoring north of Johnson City in his Lincoln Continental. Even as he sped back to the ranch, he snatched up his radio-telephone and began a long night of crisis calls—to Defense Secretary Robert McNamara for a reading on the defense implications, to OEP chief Buford Ellington for a check on contingency arrangements, to White House staffer Joseph Califano with orders that he contact officials in the blackout belt and that he "make sure we give 'em anything we can give 'em."

Before the night was out, LBJ had fired a memo to Federal Power Commission [FPC] chairman Joseph Swidler, ordering a full-scale inquiry into why the blackout had happened—and how another could be prevented. Swidler had been scheduled to retire this week, but a bulletin-board notice announcing his farewell press conference was scratched out in red and marked "canceled" by the time newsmen checked in at FPC next day. While FBI agents and other investigators spread out to prowl the grid for clues—and various state agencies launched their own inquiries—Swidler summoned the region's electrical power elite to Washington for close questioning. The investigators, he confessed, "may never trace just where it started"—but they plainly meant to try.

Had it started with an act of sabotage? Rumors of foul play flared everywhere—but the government quickly concluded that sabotage was not involved. There *was* a nervous moment at the Pentagon when the first reports came in. But a quick check showed that all Strategic Air Command and North American Air Defense Command bases were in full operation—those in the blackout area on reserve power. Nor were there any danger flashes on the Pentagon's bomb-alert boards. Topsiders flatly denied reports that the nation's military footing had been escalated, even momentarily, from its peacetime DefCon (for Defense Condition) Five posture.

"Sure, you get tense when you hear that there's been a widespread power failure in a large part of the country," said one Pentagon official. "You can't rule out an attack or sabotage, so you make some quick checks. But you don't go into any alert condition or flush your SAC bombers or start cranking up missiles like you see in the movies."

"Got a Match?"

Yet it did have, for moments that turned to hours, the quality of a science-fiction thriller; it was the night when, to all appearances, the world stood still. The lights spluttered out in Boston just as inventor Richard R. Walton finished rewiring a complicated electrical gadget in his basement workshop. "Sorry," he called upstairs to his wife. In Conway, N.H., 11-year-old Jay Hounsell idly picked up a stick and swatted a telephone pole—and the lights went out. He ran fearfully home to his mother to confess. A Toronto man was talking long distance to a friend in New York when the blackout began. "Hey," said the New Yorker incredulously moments later, "the lights just went out here, too." In Manhattan, a Consolidated Edison electrical worker groped his way out of a suddenly darkened power substation, stopped a passing CBS newsman and asked sheepishly: "Got a match?"

It was only the beginning of the agonizing hours in the streets and skyscrapers and subways of the Megalopolis. Authorities called up National Guardsmen, off-duty cops, auxiliary police, civil-defense workers and civilian volunteers as a hedge against widespread disorders that never materialized—and kept them on for rescue errands and traffic duty. The only serious outbreak was a four-hour, furniture-wrecking riot by 320 prisoners at the Walpole, Mass., penitentiary; it was squelched by state cops with tear gas. There were scores of auto accidents, most of them no more than minor bumps in the snail-paced traffic (though a Long Island City bus did plow into a crowd of pedestrians at a bus stop, bowling over more than 30 and hospitalizing nine). And crime rates throughout the region fell well below normal.

"It's OK, Honey"

Far more often, the wary Megalopolitans startled themselves pleasantly at how well they could behave in a pinch. The night was not without its plain venality; hucksters in New York sold 15-cent candles for $1 each, 59-cent flashlights for $2.50, cigarettes for 75 cents a pack, short cab rides for $15. But the real keynote was struck by a Negro cleaning woman who shepherded a Manhattan career girl up ten flights of stairs to her apartment, lent her two candles, and waved away a $5 tip. "It's OK, honey," she said. "Tonight, everyone helps everyone."

And so it seemed through a night of sudden emergencies and makeshift solutions, of momentary fear and lingering camaraderie. Utility crews worked through the night trying to get The System going again—a laborious effort that required disengaging each local power net from the big grid, firing up banked boilers and reactivating dead generators. So the Megalopolitans waited, improvised and bantered. And they endured.

They endured even near-miss brushes with disaster—a peril that was nowhere so painfully real as at the airports whose radios, beacons and radar went suddenly dead. Three planes were coming in, minutes apart, at New York's Kennedy International Airport when New York literally disappeared beneath them. "We turned right," one pilot reported, "and everything was gone." In the tower, a traffic controller found himself talking uselessly into a mute radio: "It was like a dream in which you open your mouth to say something and no sound comes out." Aides scrambled around, found flashlights, got a battery-run radio working in time to warn the planes away. Albany's airport control tower sent out an SOS for emergency vehicles to light one runway; the tower, with a portable radio unit, talked down five planes in two hours. Scores of airliners were diverted or grounded. In New York, airlines turned their grounded jets over to stranded passengers, fed them, showed them movies, invited them to bed down in their seats.

Medics

Hospitals switched to emergency generators when they could, flashlights and candles when they could not. At Albany's Medical Center Hospital, attendants reassured one nervously expectant father: "Don't worry, the doctor can deliver a baby in the dark." He did, aided by candle and flashlight—a 7-pound boy. At St. Luke's in New York, after another blackout delivery, an official confessed: "I can't tell you if it's a girl or a boy." At St. Vincent's in Greenwich Village, iron lungs stopped working; a distress call brought 30 volunteer pumpers from a nearby coffeehouse that was scarcely dimmer than normal. Bellevue Hospital doctors finished a successful cornea transplant under battery lamps. At the Bronx municipal hospital, an anesthesiologist broke from a blacked-out surgical suite, groped down seven flights to fetch flashlights, climbed up again in time for surgeons to complete a lung-removal operation. The patient lived—and under the circumstances, said one perspiring doctor afterward, "that makes the operation a roaring success."

Traffic slowed to a crawl in city after city—and turned passing pedestrians into surprisingly effective amateur traffic cops. Businessmen shucked their briefcases in Toronto and helped unglue a record traffic jam, compounded when streetcars and trolley buses carrying some 48,000 passengers ran dead. A 14-year-old Boy Scout lent a semaphore-trained hand in Providence. Students piled out of Boston's Back Bay dormitories and joined cops togged in dinner jackets (for the blacked-out policemen's ball) at clogged intersections. A brown-cassocked Franciscan friar steered traffic at one Manhattan crossing, actor Tony Perkins at another, a banker and a bootblack together at a third.

Motor Pool

With the subways out and cabs at a premium, New Yorkers hiked or hitched or hopped onto the back bumpers of overloaded buses. They even offered one another lifts, only occasionally at a price.

("Where ya going?" an off-duty chauffeur in on-duty livery asked a couple outside Midtown Manhattan's Americana Hotel. "LaGuardia Airport," they replied. "Fifty bucks," said the chauffeur—whereupon the couple climbed aboard without complaint.)

The subway breakdowns hit at the very peak of the homeward rush. Only Boston's MBTA lines escaped; they ran on, as usual, on their own power. Toronto's stoppage was merely a massive inconvenience, with 12,000 riders stuck underground for up to an hour. But New York's was a cosmic snafu. A few of the stranded 600,000 sat up all night in packed, steamy, sooty cars that had herked and jerked and died under the streets, on elevated tracks and bridges, or beneath the rivers. Yet they sat patiently, even good-humoredly, until transit workers and guardsmen led them out of the trains, into the forbiddingly dark tunnels and down narrow trackside catwalks to safety. Men yielded their seats to ladies; and the ladies, on one stalled train, offered them back. On another, a woman fainted on a forward car; the word buzzed back to another woman, who produced a bottle of smelling salts, started it up hand-to-hand to the stricken stranger. Manfully grinning conductors prowled the cars, calling, "How's everybody?" To everybody's surprise, everybody answered, "Fine!"

High above the streets, too, office workers were marooned at their desks—or in more than 200 elevators suddenly frozen between floors. At Rochester's Our Lady of Mercy convent, a rescue worker wedged open a stalled elevator, found an elderly nun with heart trouble kneeling in prayer over her rosary beads. Manhattanites were caged for up to seven hours before firemen smashed through walls to free them. Nine men and a woman were sealed for five hours in a stuffy, 6-by-6 elevator in a no-exit express shaft in one Wall Street tower. The building engineer—himself stranded in a Hoboken-bound train under the Hudson River—groped a mile out of the tube, took a ferry back to Manhattan, found his way to the building, helped rescue workers break through a washroom wall into the shaft and pluck the ten to safety.

Interlude

Thirteen elevators—and 96 passengers—were caught in the lofty reaches of the Empire State Building alone. The prisoners formed a Blackout Club in one, played word games in another. Firemen broke into a third, asked the passengers: "Are there any pregnant women in this car?" A man's voice came back: "We've hardly even met."

Many office workers simply stayed put in the sky until the work or the liquor ran out. Some, like former U.S. Sen. Kenneth Keating on the 52nd floor of the Pan-Am Building, simply bedded down where they were. Others walked down pitchy stairwells—among them the United Nations' U Thant, with two candles, from his 38th-floor Secretariat office. Thousands of others had to walk *up*—including a squadron of firemen who struggled to the 36th floor of the Pan-Am Building, only to discover that the "fire" there had started in a wastebasket and died out before they arrived.

The streets below were aswarm with the marooned, queued up at bus stops and pay phones, hunting up restaurants and saloons, or simply taking the brisk night air and enjoying the spectacle of a city suddenly gone dark save only for a spectacularly full moon and a million flickering candles. Thousands sprawled on the floor at Grand Central and Penn Stations, draped themselves over chairs in candlelit hotel lobbies, snuggled in display furniture at department stores, curled up in pews at St. Patrick's Cathedral, napped on armory cots. The posh Four Seasons was a soup kitchen for the night, dishing up free bowls of black-bean soup. At Gimbels a clerk climbed on a counter with a guitar and struck up, "When the lights go on again all over the world . . ." A Saks Fifth Avenue buyer made a bed of $100 cashmere sweaters. Forty wayfarers bedded down at the Simmons mattress showroom. An NYU coed was strolling upper Broadway when suddenly a subway grating heaved open; a trapped transit rider pulled himself out, dusted himself off and asked mildly: "Excuse me, but how do I get to CCNY?" The answer: walk north—50 blocks.

New Yorkers, who are at the center of Megalopolis, have a deep well of fatalism about The System; they rather expect it to betray them, and they reacted at first with their customary irritation toward Con Ed, the chief electricity supplier for New York. But irritation soon turned to empathy at the enormity of Con Ed's recovery problems—and wonderment at the dimensions of the blackout. ("Hey, it's all over—Rochester, Syracuse, Boston," announced one Village pub crawler. "They can't pinpernt it!") Transistors drew little knots of people everywhere; only radio mastered the communications collapse that blacked out TV, reduced wire-service tickers to last clatters of gibberish, and knocked out all morning papers except the Times (which borrowed The

Newark Evening News presses and turned out a ten-page edition by candlelight). Radio—and the resilience of the telephone system—clearly helped to avert any incipient panic.

For the very young and the very old, it remained a fearful night—but numberless others in between seemed to be enjoying themselves. Some drank and sang and necked in the streets; parties of Frenchmen and U.S. Southerners stranded on the Empire State Building's 86th-floor observation roof chorused one another with "La Marseillaise" and "Dixie." Strangers helped one another in the dark, sent thank-you notes and flowers next morning. A blind woman led passengers out of one subway station; a church sexton handed out votive candles on the streets.

Do It Again

The Great White Way went black, but pianist Vladimir Horowitz played on through Chopin's finger-tripping "Polonaise Fantasy" before a rehearsal audience at Carnegie Hall, and an off-Broadway show went on, by candlelight, to a gallery of seven people and two dogs. Folk singer Bob Dylan sat in a Village bistro pondering the gloom through dark glasses and announced: "I've been expecting this all along." But there was a tingle in the air, a sense of discovery born in the night and nurtured through countless story-swapping sessions the morning after. "They should do this more often," enthused a 19-year-old girl, en route home after a ballet lesson in the dark. "Everyone is much more friendly. It's a big community again—people have time to stop and talk."

But the experience was also sobering for the Megalopolitans— a rather unsettling lesson in how totally their lives are wired to electricity. The big blackout stopped not only factories but dentists' drills, not only subways but Mixmasters, not only lights but clocks and cash registers, X-rays and milking machines, water pumps and hair driers, stock tickers and stereo sets, doorbells and discotheques. Electricity had become to a stunning extent the main current of American civilization, and one measure was New York's hangover the morning after Black Tuesday. Three of Con Ed's generators were damaged and still out of service; commuter trains were left at the wrong ends of their lines; perhaps 30 per cent of the city's work force never showed up for work, and half those who did were sent home early as a hedge against overloading The System anew.

What's Up?

In the numb aftermath, all the wonder and worry and anger could be distilled into the single anguished question posed by Providence Mayor Joseph A. Doorley Jr.: "How the hell could something like that happen in this day and age?" If anything, the answer was even more chilling: no one really knew. Public- and private-utility experts could easily recite the effects—the falling-domino wave produced by a sudden drain somewhere in the system—but not the proximate cause. In the early hours, first one, then another spot in Upstate New York was singled out as the root of the power failure—only to bring swift denials from one or another of the companies that serve the area.

Amid the confusion, Washington's own unpreparedness to deal with a crisis short of nuclear war was clear as day. "If this had been an attack," said one OEP hand, "we would have had at our fingertips the three telephone numbers of the men who could tell us all the particulars about that power grid. As it was, I charged all over town trying to fine *one* of them." In the aftermath, OEP was doing "a lot of reviewing" of its contingency operations.

Probing

There would be a lot of investigating, too, by Federal, regional, and state authorities. U.S. Sen. Warren Magnuson promised a probe by his Senate Commerce Committee: "The security, welfare and safety of the people have been placed in jeopardy. We must be certain it does not occur again—anywhere." Rep. Walter Rogers, named to lead a House committee inquiry, was sore at the power elite for reassuring Congress that no such breakdown could happen. "Well," snorted Rogers, "somebody was mistaken, because it has happened." His off-the-cuff remedy: not one but two emergency back-up systems.

For his own part, the FPC's Swidler pressed phlegmatically on with his inquiry, posing a nineteen-point questionnaire to representatives of the region's power companies, acknowledging at the outset that they might "never all agree on precisely what happened." But that was only part of Swidler's Presidential charter. What had happened to the supposed safeguards built into the interlocking system? Should the grid arrangement be changed in some way? Should the government move in—with, say, increased muscle to force member companies of power grids to remedy weaknesses in their nets? LBJ wanted fast answers—and Swidler pressed to deliver them this week.

Freak

The prevailing view among utility men was that the blackout was a freak that simply shouldn't have happened. And yet regional failures *had* happened before—notably a five-state Midwest blackout that blanketed four times as much territory (though it affected only a tenth as many people, and for far shorter times). And some thought it could happen again—that the day might come when a failure in an interwoven nationwide grid could black out the entire U.S. within moments. The problem was that the grid system is efficient and economical when it works, however disastrous the results when it doesn't. "Power interconnections are a wonderful thing from the economic viewpoint," said one utility man, "but the more we get, the more exposure we have to a major failure."

For the moment, in the Megalopolis, it was enough that the lights were blazing, the subways and streetcars rolling, the elevators going up and down, the water pumping, the clocks telling time, the shavers shaving, the tickers ticking, the refrigerators rumbling. It had been tough but not intolerable the night they turned civilization off. Now civilization was working again. Black Tuesday had been an epiphany of the push-button age, a demonstration of the final vulnerability of the mightiest society on earth. Could it happen again? Maybe so, maybe not—but now it was a memory that all the lights in all the cities could not dim.

The Draft Resisters

By Chandler Brossard

The war in Vietnam brought protesters and draft resisters into the streets of America in droves. From angry crowds to student-organized marches to public immolation, U.S. citizens exercised their freedoms of speech, assembly, and protest in an unprecedented manner. Draft resisters violated federal law and risked imprisonment by publicly burning their draft cards as a way of denouncing both the war and the draft. Students descended on college campuses to march and chant in an effort to express their adamant dissatisfaction with the war in Vietnam. However, many Americans found the antiwar sentiment, and the passionate protests that it produced, baffling and frightening. Some claimed that the protests were organized by Communist sympathizers. Others believed that the protesters themselves were illiterate and uneducated and only protested the war because they were incapable of understanding its importance. Senior editor of *Look* magazine, Chandler Brossard reviewed the protests of 1965 from the perspective of those who organized the antiwar movement and those who opposed it. Through his synopsis and the words of prominent figures on both sides of the protests, it is clear that the Vietnam War further disturbed the already unsettled peace within the United States.

Few military involvements in our history have brought forth such massive, organized protests as the war in Vietnam. And no other dissent has been met with such official rage and counterattack as the action of 1965's "resisters." The cries and accusations from both sides, those supporting the demonstrators and those condemning them, would indicate that the issues may be deeper than the war in Vietnam and whether or not to resist the military draft. The value and moral structure of each group seem at stake, and this struggle, now that it has been launched so vigorously, could continue for a long time and could permanently affect the social-political structure of the United States.

Reactions to the Resisters

The majority of the draft and war protesters, those, at least, who have taken part in the marches and rallies throughout the country, are of college age, the "younger generation." A large number of them, however, are older; they represent another generation, but are sympathetic in values and goals. The "Get out of Vietnam" exhibitions have been going on for some time and are, in a way, a continuation of the "Stay away from Cuba" demonstrations that originated during the Kennedy Administration. The antidraft movement is relatively new and has coincided with the escalation of the conflict in Vietnam.

Criticism of the protesters has come from every quarter, and so has agreement with many of their views and feelings. They have been denounced by church groups and applauded by individual church spokesmen. They have been attacked in a personal way by some newspapers as "bearded bums," members of an "acne alliance," who dress in a dirty and strange way. Some congressmen have charged that their demonstrations have demoralized our troops in Vietnam. Other observers, both military and civilian, recently on that scene, insist that the demonstrators have not been taken seriously by the troops and that troop morale is good. High Administration officials have stated that these rallies and marches are giving America a bad reputation abroad, yet the international response, some observers contend, has been generally positive because the demonstrations give the impression of America being a peaceful, not aggressive, country.

Washington's Response

The response from high official quarters has varied in tenor from absurdity and hysteria and threats to well-modulated tones of analysis and dissent. Former President Dwight D. Eisenhower characterized the anti-war groups in a nonpolitical way. He called them "beatniks"; he deplored the fact that "the girls are just as bad—hair stringing down over their faces"; he suggested that perhaps one way to bring the young males to their senses would be for "the girls to turn their backs on boys like that." "Sloppy dress," Mr. Eisenhower said, indicates "sloppy thinking."

President Eisenhower's statements showed a certain amount of almost parental concern and disappointment, but hope. Outbursts from members of Congress have, at least in some cases, been of another order entirely. Rep. L. Mendel Rivers (D., S.C.), chairman of the House Armed Services Committee, charged that the Americans who were protesting our war policy were "filthy buzzards and vermin," who ought to be arrested. The reaction of Sen. Richard B. Russell (D., Ga.) to the protesters was of a more complex nature and had to do with civil rights as well: ". . . I have said on the floor of the Senate that the fact that people in high places had encouraged campaigns of civil disobedience throughout this land in other cases would bring home, at other times, under other conditions, campaigns of civil disobedience that would be much more far-reaching and dangerous than those they had encouraged.

"One sure effect of these campaigns and demonstrations will be to prolong the war in Vietnam. . . . As for the young men taking part in these demonstrations, some of them are pathetic because they are being misled by wily agitators."

The response of Senate minority leader Everett M. Dirksen was in a similar vein. "The spectacle of young men," he stated, "willing to perjure themselves to avoid the draft and willing to let the world know that they do not support other young Americans arrayed in battle in Vietnam in the cause of freedom is enough to make any person loyal to his country weep."

That these demonstrators, especially those coming out against the draft, which beckons nearly all of the young men, are *ipso facto* wrong in any of their views or feelings is the opinion of many in high places. These officials feel that protests are automatically a threat to national unity.

A Diverse Group

Yet Lt. Gen. Lewis B. Hershey, director of Selective Service, in an exclusive statement to *Look*, says, "Every generation has its small minority who are perpetual adolescents. Nowadays, many of them are on the college campus, where they are easily misled and misguided by, probably, their counterparts from somewhat older generations. We've become a very permissive people in recent years."

It would be difficult to estimate the number of college students and other young people (to say nothing of the much older people) who feel sympathetic to the war and draft protesters. According to one estimate, more than 100,000 people throughout the country marched in the various anti-war parades and rallies. (Untallied thousands of anti-antiwar marchers have paraded, 25,000 in Manhattan alone.) Represented in the anti-war demonstrations were some 40 different groups. Among them: the Catholic Peace Fellowship, Students for a Democratic Society, Women Strike for Peace, Youth Against War and Fascism, the Student Nonviolent Coordinating Committee, the War Resisters League, the Northern Student Movement. Roughly half the 10,000 marchers in New York City were women.

The number and diverseness of these groups would make one seriously examine the allegations made by several Government officials that the movement is Communist-inspired and manipulated. It is undoubtedly true that some Communist party members are involved, but they very likely have been involved to the same degree in the civil-rights movement and labor movement as well. But the greatest number of protesters, it would seem, are engaged for nonpolitical, nonreligious reasons. They are reacting, as one of them has said, "for moral and humanistic reasons."

Healthy Dissent

The protesters do have their advocates, and their statements suggest much more than just a concern with the war and the draft. There is, for example, this statement from Prof. John K. Galbraith of Harvard University, former ambassador to India, that student protests against the war "are proper, good and desirable." Over 50 university professors went along with this view in a signed statement. From Sen. Gale W. McGee (D., Wyo.), a former professor, comes this comment: "As one who has vigorously defended America's tough line in Vietnam, perhaps I may be permitted to say that we must not destroy our fundamental freedoms in the name of preserving them. This we threaten to do if we ban the pickets or smear them as Communists. I am sure there must be some Communists in the ranks. . . . But I deplore labeling every protest movement as Communist-inspired because of that. This smears the overwhelming majority of the protesters in a way detrimental to their free right to object, or to oppose."

Sen. Wayne Morse (D., Ore.) goes further: "The near hysteria with which these demonstrations are being met by Government officials suggests that they are anxious to tag all dissent as lawless, reckless and bordering on sedition.

"To bring the full weight of Government police power down upon a few noticeable individuals can, they hope, spread disrepute to the whole idea of dissent or objection to a policy in Vietnam that is producing not peace, but only war and the prospect of more war."

One congressman who, like some others approached by LOOK for comments, did not want to be identified, said, apropos the new law making it a Federal crime, punishable by up to five years in jail and a fine

Many people denounced the draft and the war by protesting.

of up to $10,000, to burn a draft card: "This is a truly absurd law and punishment. It shows real rage and fear. Something like 60 days in jail or a much, much smaller fine would be more like a reasonable idea."

Dissent Hysteria

Some anti-resisters have accused those in "the movement," as it is sometimes called, of being semiliterates, hysterics who don't know fact from fantasy. However, here is what one senator's office had to say about them: "They are very bright and very well informed. They really know their facts. They're a hell of a lot more knowledgeable on the war situation, and politics in general, than half the people on the Hill. When they come around here, I get the terrible feeling that I haven't done my homework well. This generation is lots more sophisticated and involved than my own. They are determined to have a hand in forging their destiny. They won't sit numbly by."

Among those on the Hill who share the anti-war view of our involvement in Vietnam is Sen. Ernest Gruening (D., Alaska). He has said, "I oppose U.S. policies in Vietnam . . . not alone because they are unrealistic and are leading us down the path to a full-scale major war, but also because they are playing right into the hands of Chinese-imperialist communism." He declared, too, "Our actions in South Vietnam have tarnished our image before the world as a law-abiding nation." And, on another occasion: "We must also recognize, which the President has deliberately failed to recognize, that this is a civil war, the control of which does not rest in the capital of North Vietnam or in Communist China. . . ."

Still another congressional office—which asked not to be identified, "because this is a very sensitive area, and one can risk a lot by speaking out critically"—stated that: "The President seems to have a morbid fear of these kids. If he really doesn't take them seriously, why is he so disturbed?"

One observer had this to say about the accusation that the marchers were prolonging the war by giving the Reds false hopes of a U.S. collapse: "Nonsense. Everybody knows that the marchers really are not going to influence foreign policy at this point. And Ho Chi Minh is much too realistic to think America is in a state of revolt."

Forms of Resistance

Now for the protesters themselves. There have been some extreme gestures that, because of their dramatic quality, have been played up by the daily press and, consequently, have been publicly regarded as reflecting a general lawlessness in the entire movement. Anti-war protesters have burned themselves to death. Several young men have publicly destroyed their draft cards. About a dozen others have refused to be inducted into the armed forces and have been jailed for it. A group based in New York City has reportedly made plans to send money and food to the Vietcong. A handful of dissenters in California and New York City have issued "guides" for beating the draft by a variety of dissemblances. Listed on one such guide was advice on how to "play" homosexual, be an epileptic, fake an allergy, and play addict and alcoholic. But such antics seem to enjoy a limited action in the overall movement.

The majority of the protesters have embraced a program of legal conscientious objection. If the draft boards agree, upon examining their forms 150, that they are indeed CO's, then that is that. If they are denied this classification, most of them seem willing, however reluctantly, to accept the consequences. Few have indicated that they would refuse to be inducted and then to go to jail.

Only two of all the groups have become organized on a national scale. They are the Students for a Democratic Society, based in Chicago, and the National Coordinating Committee to End the War in Vietnam, with headquarters in Madison, Wis. The SDS claim to have 80 chapters throughout the country and a dues-paying membership of about 3,000 that is gradually rising. It was the Coordinating Committee, under a 22-year-old University of Wisconsin graduate named Frank Emspak, that organized the national peace marches on October 15 and 16. The Department of Justice is reportedly investigating both organizations. These groups preach for legal conscientious objection. It is safe speculation that both groups, because of their student appeal and their sense of organization, will be around for some time, long after local groups, which sprang up just in connection with the war and draft problems and which do not have an overall program, have disappeared. The SDS, for example, has already launched a program of reaching high-school students and instructing them in the various issues involved and, quite likely, in all the views and stands of what is now called "the new Left."

Defining Their Values

What do these young people believe? What are their values? It's best to let them speak for themselves. Carl Oglesby, president of the SDS, is 30 years old and a graduate of the University of Michigan. He says: "I deeply believe in my country as much as President Johnson says he does. But I want it to stop practicing things, all over the world, that are contrary to its greatness, contrary to what Thomas Jefferson believed, contrary to what the American Revolution was all about. I believe America has become warped by a few powerful Government people who fundamentally do not believe in or practice the ideas upon which our country was founded. When I hear what various congressmen and others in the Government call us—beatniks, cowards, traitors—I feel pain, not anger. They do not understand us, they have not tried to understand us intelligently. I want more than anything to talk with them, to keep in touch with them. Unhappily, I feel that President Johnson is totally inaccessible.

"I think that you have to imagine that the world is flat, not round, and in the center of this great flat world there is a big volcano sticking up, and everybody in the world lives under that volcano, except the people in the United States, who are living on the volcano."

Oglesby's co-resister and national secretary of SDS is a 22-year-old graduate of Swarthmore College named Paul Booth. His feelings about the cultural and political scene he puts in the following way: "The entire culture, its ideas and positions and values, needs rehabilitating, and this is what we are up to and dedicated to continuing. It is a new kind of job, you could say. There is no political orientation as such behind it. No Communist manipulation, as people have charged. I think that part of the general reaction against the marches and protests is that this sort of thing is somehow against the American grain. I mean, to a public that has become so accustomed to being manipulated and directed, it is very difficult to understand a movement like ours that comes out of a spontaneous moral indignation that is not manipulated or directed by something outside it. For instance, the President feels threatened by us."

Whatever one may feel, morally and politically, about the war issue, the following elements of the anti-war, draft-resister scene are clear: The charges of Communist direction are founded more on emotion than research: it is unlikely that the marches are prolonging the war or influencing North Vietnam policy: it is not true that all the protesters are anarchistic riffraff.

A Generation on the Move

This may well be a historic moment. For the first time, political or ideological thinking has left the theoretical sphere, among the mass of intelligentsia, and entered the bloodstream of action. This new group, the American college-age critics and dissenters, could become a continuing force.

An academic view of the movement is expressed by Dr. Edgar Z. Friedenberg, social scientist and professor of sociology at the University of California: "What is new is that a growing, though still a very small, proportion of American young people is becoming ashamed of compromise on issues that seem to them to be crucial, and this does impose a strain on our usual modes of political accommodation, which have come to depend on it, but the increased moral stature of the young people seems to me a more important gain.

"One fact that is often overlooked is that most of the college students who have been active in protest movements are among the better students and those in positions of intellectual leadership on their own campuses. Certainly these are not people with a record of failure and disaffection in the system. . . . They have developed unusual moral courage."

The generation that has been accused of massive indifference is on the move, the minority demonstrators and the majority counterdemonstrators. Every area of American society could be affected, and not just superficially, by this militant youth action. The "Age of Apathy" may be over.

CHRONOLOGY

January 4: In his State of the Union address, President Lyndon B. Johnson presents his plans for the "Great Society," including programs to fight illness, poverty, discrimination, and illiteracy.

January 16: Eighteen people are arrested in connection with the murder of three civil rights workers in Mississippi.

January 27: In South Vietnam, the civilian-led government of Tran Van Huong is ousted by military leaders in Saigon.

February 1: Martin Luther King Jr. and 770 civil rights workers are arrested during a civil rights march organized to protest voter discrimination in Alabama.

February 19: Fourteen antiwar protesters are arrested after blocking the doors to the United Nations building in New York.

February 21: Malcolm X is assassinated by a Black Muslim while speaking at an Afro-American Unity rally in New York.

March 2: The "Rolling Thunder" air campaigns begin when 150 U.S. and South Vietnamese planes bomb bases in North Vietnam.

March 7: Led by Martin Luther King Jr., civil rights activists attempt to march from Selma, Alabama, to Montgomery, Alabama, to protest unfair voting laws; protesters get only as far as Pettus Bridge, Alabama, before they are beaten and attacked with tear gas by Alabama police; the tragic event is dubbed "Bloody Sunday."

March 8: Marines land in Vietnam as part of the first deployment of American troops to the country.

March 9: King makes a second attempt to lead protesters across Pettus Bridge; Reverend James Reeb is killed by militant residents of Selma, Alabama.

March 18: Taking a definitive lead in the space race, Soviet cosmonaut Aleksei Leonov conducts the world's first space walk; he spends twenty minutes outside the Soviet spacecraft *Voskhod 2*.

March 23: American astronauts Virgil I. Grissom and John W. Young man the first U.S. two-person spaceflight on *Gemini 3*.

March 26: Led by King, twenty-five thousand civil rights activists march on the state capital in Montgomery, Alabama, to protest discrimination against black voters.

April 28: Civil war breaks out in the Dominican Republic; twenty-two thousand eight hundred U.S. troops are sent to help the Organization of American States (OAS) negotiate a cease-fire and prevent a Communist coup.

June 3: Astronaut Edward White completes the first American space walk during the flight of *Gemini 4*.

June 8: President Lyndon B. Johnson commits U.S. forces to combat in Vietnam, marking the commencement of full-scale warfare by the United States against the Vietcong guerrillas and the North Vietnamese.

July 14: The first pictures of Mars from a spacecraft are taken by the American space probe *Mariner 4*.

July 30: As part of his "Great Society," President Johnson signs the Medicare bill into law.

August 6: President Johnson signs the Voting Rights Act of 1965; the law bans unfair requirements, including literacy tests, in determining voter eligibility.

August 11: A riot erupts in the Watts neighborhood of Los Angeles. The violence continues for six days. Widespread looting, thirty-four deaths, and almost four thousand arrests are blamed on the riot.

August 29: The U.S. spacecraft, *Gemini 5*, lands in the Atlantic after eight days in space.

September 19: Cesar Chavez and the National Farm Workers Association join the Agricultural Workers Organizing Committee in a strike against unfair labor practices in Delano, California.

September 30: President Johnson signs legislation for the establishment of the National Foundation for the Arts and the Humanities.

November 9: A series of power failures causes a blackout in New York City and nine eastern states, the worst power outage in U.S. history; some affected areas are without power for more than thirteen hours; twenty-two-year-old Roger Allen LaPorte kills himself in front of the United Nations building in New York City in protest against the Vietnam War.

December 21: Four antiwar protesters are arrested in New York for burning draft cards.

December 25: The first snowboard, or "snurfer," is invented when Sherman Poppen screws together two pairs of children's skis.

December 31: California becomes the state with the largest population in the United States.

FOR FURTHER RESEARCH

The Automobile Industry

Ralph Nader, *Unsafe at Any Speed: The Designed-in Dangers of the American Automobile.* New York: Grossman, 1965.

Thomas Whiteside, *The Investigation of Ralph Nader: General Motors vs. One Determined Man.* New York: Arbor House, 1972.

Civil Rights

Haywood Burns, "The Rule of Law in the South," *Commentary*, 1965.

Clayborne Carson, *In Struggle: SNCC and the Black Awakening of the 1960's.* Cambridge, MA: Harvard University Press, 1981.

Hugh Davis Graham, *The Civil Rights Era: Origins and Development of National Policy, 1960– 1972.* New York: Oxford University Press, 1990.

Steven F. Lawson, *Running for Freedom: Civil Rights and Black Politics in America Since 1941.* Philadelphia: Temple University Press, 1991.

Abigail Thernstrom, "The Odd Evolution of the Voting Rights Act," *Public Interest*, 1979.

Counterculture

Peter Braunstein and Michael William Doyle, eds., *Imagine Nation: The American Counterculture of the 1960s and '70s.* New York: Routledge, 2002.

Kenneth J. Heineman, *Put Your Bodies Upon the Wheels: Student Revolt in the 1960's.* Chicago: I.R. Dee, 2001.

Feminism

Alice Echols, *Shaky Ground: The 60's and Its Aftershocks.* New York: Columbia University Press, 2002.

Betty Friedan, *The Feminine Mystique.* New York: W.W. Norton, 1997.

Dawn Keetley and John Pettegrew, eds., *Public Women, Public Words: A Documentary History of American Feminism.* Madison, WI: Madison House, 2002.

The Great Society

Joseph Califano Jr., *The Triumph & Tragedy of Lyndon Johnson: The White House Years.* College Station: Texas A&M University Press, 2000.

Doris Kearns, *Lyndon Johnson and the American Dream.* New York: Harper & Row, 1976.

Sar A. Levitan and Benjamin H. Johnston, *The Job Corps: A Social Experiment That Works.* Baltimore: Johns Hopkins University Press, 1975.

Migrant Workers

Susan Ferris and Ricardo Sandoval, *The Fight in the Fields: Cesar Chavez and the Farmworkers Movement.* New York: Harcourt Brace, 1997.

Beverly Fodell, *Cesar Chavez and the United Farm Workers: A Selective Bibliography.* Detroit: Wayne State University Press, 1974.

Dana Catharine de Ruiz and Richard Larios, *La Causa: The Migrant Farmworkers' Story.* Austin, TX: Raintree Steck-Vaughn, 1993.

Sydney D. Smith, *Grapes of Conflict.* Pasadena, CA: Hope, 1987.

The Space Race

James Schefter, *The Race: The Uncensored Story of How America Beat Russia to the Moon.* New York: Doubleday, 1999.

Jon Trux, *The Space Race: From Sputnik to Shuttle: The Story of the Battle for the Heavens.* London: New English Library, 1985.

War in Vietnam and the Dominican Republic

Larry Burrows, *Vietnam.* New York: Alfred A. Knopf, 2002.

Michael S. Foley, *Confronting the War Machine: Draft Resistance*

During the Vietnam War. Chapel Hill: University of North Carolina Press, 2003.

Piero Gleijeses, *The Dominican Crisis: The 1965 Constitutionalist Revolt and American Intervention.* Baltimore: Johns Hopkins University Press, 1978.

Marc Jason, ed., *The Vietnam War on Campus: Other Voices, More Distant Drums.* Westport, CT: Praeger, 2001.

Bruce Palmer Jr., *Intervention in the Caribbean: The Dominican Crisis of 1965.* Lexington: University Press of Kentucky, 1989.

Melvin Small, *Antiwarriors: The Vietnam War and the Battle for America's Hearts and Minds.* Wilmington, DE: Scholarly Resources, 2002.

Websites

African-American Odyssey, http://memory.loc.gov. Hosted by the Library of Congress, this site provides a comprehensive look at African American history. "The Civil Rights Era" section chronologically covers the civil rights movement with time lines, photographs, and links to additional information.

The American Experience: Vietnam Online, www.pbs.org. The Vietnam Online site, hosted by PBS, offers an extensive look at the intricacies of the Vietnam War. Complete with battle time lines, photographs, weaponry guides, and a Who's Who section, the website explores all aspects of the war in Vietnam.

The Space Race, www.thespacerace.com. This site is dedicated to the U.S. space missions of the 1960s and 1970s, including all of the Mercury, Gemini, and Apollo missions. With a photo gallery, chat room, and a space encyclopedia, the website provides an exhaustive look at the people and technology behind the space race.

U.S. Department of Labor: Job Corps, www.jobcorps.org. Begun in 1965 as part of President Johnson's Great Society, the Job Corps continues today as a division of the U.S. Department of Labor. This site covers the history of the Job Corps and provides information and links about its current function.

INDEX